GIFTING TO
PEOPLE
YOU LOVE

Also By Adriane G. Berg

Your Wealth-Building Years
  Financial Planning for 18- to 38-Year-Olds

Financial Planning for Couples
  How to Work Together to Build Security and Success

The Totally Awesome Business Book for Kids
  (with Arthur Berg Bochner)

The Totally Awesome Money Book for Kids (and Their Parents)
  (with Arthur Berg Bochner)

▪ ▪ ▪
GIFTING TO
PEOPLE
YOU LOVE
▪ ▪ ▪

*The Complete Family Guide to
Making Gifts, Bequests, and
Investments for Children*

ADRIANE G. BERG

Newmarket Press

First Edition

96 97 98 99 10 9 8 7 6 5 4 3 2 1

Library of Congress Cataloging-in-Publication Data
Berg, Adriane G. (Adriane Gilda), 1948–
Gifting to people you love / Adriane G. Berg.
    p.   cm.
ISBN 1-55704-273-X
    1. Gifts—Law and legislation—United States—Popular works.
2. Gifts to minors—United States.   I. Title.
KF716.Z9B47   1996
343.7305'35—dc20
[347.303535]   96-21567
                                                                CIP

Quantity Purchases:
Companies, professional groups, clubs, and other organizations may
qualify for special terms when ordering quantities of this title. For
information, write Special Sales, Newmarket Press, 18 East 48th Street,
New York, New York 10017, call (212) 832-3575, or fax (212) 832-3629.

Manufactured in the United States of America.

From Mommy, a book for my children,
Arthur Ross Berg Bochner
and
Rose Berg Bochner.
Who else?

Contents

Preface IX

1. What Are Your Goals in Investing for Your Children and Grandchildren? *1*
2. Everything You Wanted to Know About Taxing Your Children's Assets But Were Afraid to Find Out *10*
3. Titling Accounts: The Joint Account *22*
4. Titling Accounts: The Uniform Gifts to Minors Act *28*
5. Trusts *33*
6. Trust Provisions of Special Interest to Parents and Grandparents *44*
7. Selecting Trustees *48*
8. The Child's Trust *58*
9. The Family Limited Partnership *67*
10. Power of Attorney *70*
11. A Short Course on the Cost of College *74*
12. Investing for Children *88*
13. College-Specific Investments and Lump-Sum Planning *99*
14. Insurance to Build an Inheritance *108*
15. Small Gifts *117*
16. Making Your Child a Successful Beneficiary *122*
17. The Financial Rewards of Grandparenthood *134*
18. Gifting and Support Issues When Parents Divorce *146*

Appendix A: Your Child's Tax *161*
Appendix B: Children's Trust Agreement *163*
Appendix C: Certificate of the Jones Family Limited Partnership *169*
Appendix D: Power of Attorney *171*
Appendix E: Acknowledgments for Wills and Trusts *175*
Bibliography *177*
Index *179*
An Open Invitation *189*
About the Author *190*

Preface

If you are interested in this book, you have a happy problem! You have both love and money. All you need to do is get the money you have to the people you love in the right way. That doesn't sound so hard, does it? What can go wrong that such "gifts of love" warrant an entire book? *Plenty!*

As host of *The Money Show* on WABC, a radio call-in format, I often hear about the problems and concerns of loving families who have money to preserve and share for the future. Many of my listeners originally came here from other countries, to achieve the old-fashioned American Dream of getting their children a good education and a life that realizes their potential. I thrill to letters I sometimes get from parents that thank me for financial advice that helped them get the first-ever college graduate in the family through college.

But other letters arrive in my mailbox, too. Like this one from Martha and Richard Howell:

Dear Adriane:
We want to ask you if there is anything we can do for our son. He just graduated from medical school. To help pay, he took a loan that his advisor said would be

perfect because he wouldn't have to pay it back until he graduated. Now, we found out that interest was compounding on the unpaid balance and the unpaid interest, all through school. He has already paid over $30,000 on a $40,000 loan and still has $71,000 left to pay. The interest keeps compounding and he feels he will have to pay all his life. Some people say he should go into bankruptcy. He feels very despondent at a time that he should be thriving in his new profession. Is there anything we can do?

The fact is that middle-class America is tied up in knots over college financing. Special consultants, insurance companies, banks, and the government are all in the help-pay-for-college business. Some of us faithfully feed our trusty fifty-dollars-a-month savings plan; others try to make an end run with risky investments two years before C-Day. But whatever we do, paying for college education isn't easy. Oddly enough, the more money we have, the harder it may be to pay, unless we are among the very rich.

College planning isn't the only gift of love that can cause trouble. *In the next five years the average baby boomer will inherit $90,000 from their parents.* Put another way: *More than one trillion dollars will change hands intergenerationally —the largest transfer of wealth in human history!*

Do you know where your inheritance is?

Sally Cohen, one of my listeners, knows where her inheritance is. Or was. It was in the dishwasher. After her mother's funeral, Sally decided to pay tribute to her mom by washing the dishes. It was always a joke between them. Mom was a great housekeeper, but Sally—well, Sally wasn't. So with nostalgic tears in her eyes, Sally turned on the washer. She heard a clatter. Jewelry, stock certificates, even cash, were being torn apart by the machine. Mom had stashed at least $50,000 worth of securities (they never found all of them) in the washer for safekeeping. She had tried to tell Sally about it a few times, but Sally had been too busy to listen, and Mom was reluctant to make a big deal out of it. It's hard to communicate about these things.

The fact is that American wealth is about to undergo a quiet revolution. Most revolutions are about the redistribution of wealth from one group to another or to the government. In the next five years, more than one trillion dollars will change hands from one generation to another. Some family members will benefit; others will suffer. Millions will go to lawyers for court battles over this money, and billions (as much as 55 percent) will go to the government for estate taxes. All this will happen with neither a whimper nor a bang, but with the silence of denial that cloaks issues of mortality.

If you will indulge me, just one more letter:

Dear Adriane:
I am a 73-year-old woman who just got out of the hospital. I have $25,000 in the bank and my Social Security. That's all. When I came out I found that the bank won't let me have my money. A creditor of my son did something to the account and I can't get my money. I put the account in my name with my son just before I went to the hospital. Now, they say it's his money too and they can take it. Is this true? I can't afford a lawyer. What can I do?

Don't be concerned—our lady got her money back, but only because of a sympathetic judge and lots of time and attention paid to the case. Unfortunately, this sickbed story often gets repeated. Creditors, spouses, tax authorities—all can get part of a gift, whether the giver intends it or not. You must be careful with titling assets and accounts and understand the consequences.

The transfers of funds that we make during our lifetime are sometimes gifts and sometimes not. We can use convenience accounts, powers of attorney, joint accounts, and all kinds of will substitutes and beneficiary designations. Choosing from among them is like mixing your own medicine. You'd better be careful and know what you're doing.

And our "happy problem" has still more complications. Special situations like disabilities, conflicts among heirs, and many more issues must be addressed.

When I first undertook the writing of this book, I regarded it as a lighter topic than the thirteen previous books I had written, most of them about investing money. But as I began to realize the effect that each generation has on the material freedom of the next, I saw the importance of the guidance I can give. Who knows what poems will be written, cures will be discovered, and mountains will be climbed because we have preserved our wealth for future generations and made our own personal gifts of love?

GIFTING TO
PEOPLE
YOU LOVE

·1·

What Are Your Goals in Investing for Your Children and Grandchildren?

This question is deceptively simple. At first blush, you may think your goals are clear. Write them down now on any handy piece of paper. What do you want to accomplish through your gift-giving? By answering this question in writing, we often find that our goals for our children conflict with our goals for ourselves. Should you invest money in your own retirement program so that you don't burden your children when you and they are older, or should you invest money in their college plan so that they can pay for school without incurring a lifetime of student loans? Do you make a will that leaves money equally to your children, or do you give extra help to the needier one? Do you keep your plans a secret, or do you share the information? Which is better for the family and safer for the money?

It is a monumental task, investing for someone you love. You likely have your hopes and your dreams for them, but they set their own goals. You are only a surrogate, a fiduciary, for them. The money will eventually be theirs to do with as they please. Parents and grandparents who make gifts of love often experience an internal tug-of-war. They want to allocate money for the benefit of another, yet they want to exercise control over how that money is spent.

From this very human contradiction between the desire to give to a loved one and the desire to keep some authority for oneself has emerged a large body of law that was once familiar only to trust and estate lawyers, professionals who traditionally served the very rich. Because of the vast amounts of money held by the wealthiest families in our country, our gifting laws deal with tax savings, conflicts among heirs, and methods of fierce asset protection that allowed the patriarch to "rule from the grave."

Times have changed, as the American middle class approaches the mass transfer of wealth from its senior members in the next half decade. From the body of law originally designed to serve the very rich, we must be able to select the techniques for giving and investing that make sense in our lives and for our families.

Our gifts of love are an indication of how far the American Dream has been realized by people like you and me. Once upon a time we would never have been concerned about gift-giving to children or investing for children. At the turn of the century, infant mortality rates among the working class were so high that just having our children survive was a blessing. For the first half of the century, most people made their financial way alone. Into the 1950s, getting our kids to college and giving them the head start they needed was enough. It's a sign of an affluent society that we now invest for our children and our grandchildren.

But with this new affluence comes new problems. Parents are left in the dark about how they should make their investments, about how they can simultaneously save for their retirement and get their kids to college. Grandparents have an even tougher time because often after they make their gift, they are no longer decision-makers in the family. Their influence is gone.

In many ways this is a unique legal reference book, with lots of deep information on each single aspect of gift-giving. At times you will require such depth—for example, if you are preparing for a visit to your lawyer to set up a trust. At other times you won't, like when cousin Mary hands you a fifty-dollar bill for little Timmy's "college fund" and you need to refresh your memory about dividend reinvestment programs.

Do you know what you want to give? and how you want to give it? and the best way to invest it? Maybe not, but what you do know is your own vision of the future, your own special dreams for the children that you love. And even though you will be reading about law and money, this book is really about love and trust.

Certified financial planners have identified five major goals in investing for children and grandchildren. Which one is the most important to you? As you are reading, prioritize them in your mind.

1. **College planning.** Today most parents are very concerned about the skyrocketing costs of college. As parents of middle-class families, it's hard to accept that our own parents had an easier time sending us to college

than we have sending our kids, even though most of us earn much more than our folks did. In many families, college planning is an intergenerational effort.

2. **Tax savings.** By giving gifts during your lifetime to children and grandchildren, you may be hoping to save income and estate taxes.

3. **A smooth inheritance.** Perhaps you are a parent or a grandparent who would like to build an inheritance for your children or grandchildren to insure their future. Or perhaps you've been lucky enough to have accumulated wealth already, and you want to pass it on in a way that is as cost- and hassle-free as possible.

4. **A nest egg.** Other than for college, you might like to accumulate money for your children for an emergency, or to start them in a business, or just to start them out a little bit wealthier in life.

5. **Investing your children's money.** Maybe you are already investing for your children with their own money. Many minors have received an inheritance, a settlement in court, or a child support settlement. Or your children may be wage-earners already. In all these cases, you want to know how to invest money for them in the safest and best way.

Which of these goals is the most important goal to you, and in which order? As you read this book, you may realize that some of your goals are in conflict. You may end up not taking action because every time you decide on a course, something else impinges on your thinking. And you may be quite right. But eventually you will have to make some decisions. The Gifts of Love Profile that follows is designed to help you clarify your intentions.

Gifts of Love Profile

The beneficiaries of my gifts are:

I favor them in this order:

I intend to gift $ to   within a period of   [months, years].

I have [a strong, a moderate, no] desire to keep investment or other control over the gift.

Tax savings is of [high, moderate, no] importance to me.

If tax savings are important, I care most about saving [income, gift, estate] tax.

The assets I will gift are in [cash, real estate, a business, stock, tangibles, other].

They [are, are not] highly appreciated from the time I acquired them.

Up until now, I have used [trusts, wills, joint accounts, custodial accounts, other] to give my gifts.

My three greatest concerns in order of their importance are:

1. _____

2. _____

3. _____

Do not reveal your thoughts to your family as yet. In all my financial-planning books, I have included numerous worksheets for the reader to complete, but none of them are to be kept so confidential as this simple Gifts of Love Profile. Your thoughts on the matter of giving may change often. You may revise your plan to the disappointment and perhaps ill feelings of some of them. Communication is important, but until you have finished this book, your gift-giving intentions are still on the drawing board and should be kept private.

Once you have decided on your goals, the most essential questions to consider in gift-giving are:

- How much should I give?
- In what form shall I give it?
- What assets shall I give?

The rest of this book will help you answer these questions.

WHAT'S YOUR GIFT-GIVING STYLE?

How much you give and the form your gift will take depends a great deal on both your goals and your gift-giving style.

Whether you know it or not, you have already developed a gift-giving style. When my clients come to my office, I have been fascinated to see how they differ. I know a grandmother who has for years "socked away" money into a low-paying bank account, without telling anyone about it. Her children have a vague notion that she may be doing this, but they would never breach family etiquette and ask her any questions.

The grandmother's idea is that she may need the money in later years herself and that giving out the information would mean she could not get the money back. For the most part, she holds this money in joint accounts or in accounts that she has access to, which are therefore not true gifts. The money remains in her control. She saves neither estate taxes nor income taxes.

At the other end of the spectrum is another grandma. Every Christmas she makes a disclosed gift of up to $10,000 to each of her grandchildren. She makes no demands on them with regard to how that money is to be used, and she does not inquire as to how her yearly gifts are being expended.

Of course, both grandmas can run into trouble. The first is in danger of being so secretive that no family member is able to keep track of their gift. Should she become incapacitated, the accounts could go unclaimed and end up being forfeited to the government. The second grandma has relinquished all control. Often her gift is used for things of which she does not approve, such as to buy a fast car or to pay off credit-card debt.

Many of my clients are parents, rather than grandparents, who would like to begin a gift-giving program, but they are confused as to what method to use. Since they are young or at most middle-aged, they would like to keep as much control as the law will permit yet they would like the money be available to their children in case of emergency.

The following chapters sort out the pros and cons of various ways of gift-giving so that you can judge which is best for yourself and your children or grandchildren. Each permits a different degree of control and disclosure. Each also has different tax consequences. But before we get too sophisticated, let's address the simplest style of all: outright gift-giving.

OUTRIGHT GIFTS

Obviously, the simplest style of gift-giving is to give the gift directly to the child. Many people do this without any policing by the government, the courts, or a fiduciary. Giving stamps, jewelry, or coins to children outright, however, contains no guarantee that the money will be invested or used in a proper way. If cash, real estate, securities, bonds, or other assets are transferred to a minor, the law itself often encourages the minor to do little more than spend the money. In most states, a minor cannot create a trust, hire a financial adviser, or even make a will. In some areas of the country, a minor cannot even rent a safe-deposit box. Further, if anything does happen to the minor, his estate will pay taxes on the amount.

Therefore, before an outright gift is made to a minor, that minor's fiscal responsibility should be considered. If the gift is substantial, thought should be given to giving the gift in trust.

Most parents and grandparents would not dream of making an actual transfer to a minor without retaining at least some control over the gift. In fact, this is not always wise. Many teenagers have great fiscal responsibility and knowledge. One of my callers loaned $20,000 to her entrepreneurial grandson, who ran a moving company. She received the money back, plus $17,000 profit. Not bad!

The point is to consider each family member separately

and try to avoid making a blanket decision for all of the children or grandchildren. You will want to make every effort to be fair. You might want to invest money for a child who is a spendthrift and transfer money outright to another who lives frugally.

·2·

Everything You Wanted to Know About Taxing Your Children's Assets But Were Afraid to Find Out

My son Arthur, at age thirteen, was the author of two books and ran a card concession at a local retail shop. It bugged him that he had to pay taxes at my high tax bracket on any interest or growth from his savings. It's hard to convince a child to sock savings away when over 37 percent of anything he earns goes for taxes. Now that Arthur is fourteen, this will change and he will get his own lower tax bracket. This may seem odd but it is the result of the so-called "kiddie tax" on earnings from a kid's investments under the age of fourteen.

We tend to resent the taxation of our children's assets even more than we resent the taxation of our own. After all, they're just kids! Can't the government leave their money alone? The answer is no. Not only are children of all ages subject to income tax, but they are presently subject to more income tax than ever. Many traditional devices used in the past to shelter their wealth have been eliminated.

Because most gift-giving and many investment decisions are tax-oriented, tax considerations will influence the way you hold money for your children (titling) and the types of investments you make. Since they are so important, let's review the types of taxes we are concerned with, then discuss each one in turn.

- **Income Tax:** Tax on children's income both from their earnings (if they work) and from investments they hold in their own name.
- **Gift Tax:** Any amount over $10,000 transferred to a beneficiary within one year must be reported by the donor on their gift tax returns for that year. The amount of tax paid will depend on several factors.
- **Estate Tax:** A tax on the wealth accumulated by a decedent at the time of his or her death. The tax is paid by the estate, not the beneficiary, according to a formula.
- **Capital Gains Tax:** A tax imposed when an asset is sold at a profit. The profit is included as part of the yearly income of the person or entity that benefited by the sale. The tax is greatly affected by the rules of "stepped-up basis." (See page 18.)

INCOME TAX

Children of any age who have earned income (income from employment) must file a tax return, and the tax is based on their own tax bracket (as if they were an adult). Children of any age who have earned income, however, can also start their own pension plan or IRA. There is no age restriction: Even an infant can start an IRA with their first $2,000 of earned income. (If you own your own business, you may prefer to give a gift to your child, not outright but by hiring him as, say, your photographic model.)

The Tax Reform Act of 1986 introduced a new tax, unofficially called the kiddie tax. It applies only to children under the age of fourteen. Children fourteen and over have their own tax bracket, like that of adults, and are not subject to the kiddie tax.

The kiddie tax is imposed only on investment income or profits earned by children *under* the age of fourteen. Children under the age of 14 who have gains or income from investments are taxed at the marginal tax rate of their parents, as if the parents had earned that investment income or capital gain.

There is an exception: The first $650 of yearly income from investments is not subject to the kiddie tax at all. The second $650 is taxed only at the child's rate, which is based on his total income that year. A child who has no earned income is probably in the low 15 percent tax bracket. That means the first $1,300 that the child earns from investments in a year is subject to a minimum tax. For every dollar over that, the child is taxed at the parent's marginal rate.

To figure whether you need to file a separate tax form for your child or use your own, see Appendix A. For investment purposes, your choice is clear. If you are in a high tax bracket, it does you no good to transfer large amounts of money in gifts to your children to save income tax. You will only save on the first $1,300 of investment income or gain earned every year. Beyond that, if your program is to save your own income tax, and your child is under the age of fourteen, keep the money, because it will be taxed at your level anyway.

Let's say you've done a good job of saving for your child's college education. Since children fourteen years and over get their own tax bracket, you might want to give your child a one-time lump-sum gift when he reaches fourteen, because the money will then accumulate at his lower tax bracket.

One time-honored tax-wise strategy is to put only enough money in your child's name to yield $1,300 or less every single year. Once that amount is reached, invest the money for him at your own discretion. Title it in your name, and then when he reaches the age of fourteen, you can transfer all the earmarked college funds over to the child.

Caveat: This strategy must be balanced against the possibility that money in his name will spoil a child's chance at getting college aid. (See Chapter 11.)

GIFT TAX

Under certain circumstances, when a gift is given, a gift tax must be paid. Although this seems odd to most people, from the government's point of view its purpose is clear. The government presumes that the very purpose of giving the gift is to avoid paying eventual estate taxes. In order to prevent people from divesting themselves of all their assets right before their death, the government imposes gift taxes, eliminating the incentive to give away your property to save estate taxes.

The Gift-Tax Exclusion

It is wise to give gifts in a way that is gift-tax free. How is this done? To begin with, anyone may give $10,000 per year per person to any number of other people without paying a gift tax. This figure of $10,000 was raised from $3,000 in 1980. Moreover, gift-splitting can increase the amount a couple can give.

Gift-Splitting

The government permits a husband and wife each to give $10,000 per beneficiary per year tax-free. One spouse, however, might have $20,000 to give to a child, while the other might not have enough to make a $10,000 gift. In such a situation, the husband and wife may give a gift of $20,000 together. The government, in effect, considers each spouse to have contributed $10,000 and in this way splits the gift. Thus husband and wife pay no gift tax, as each is considered to have given within the $10,000 limit.

Direct Gifts

Grandparents may give unlimited gifts to cover tuition or medical costs without paying a gift tax. But such payments must be made directly to the school or healthcare institution.

How Gift Tax Is Calculated

If you do give a taxable gift, you would be wise to know how much gift tax you will pay. To figure it out, you have to know the value of the gift itself. The tax is imposed on the fair market value of a noncash gift at the time when it is given (that is, what a willing buyer would pay for it and what a willing seller would accept for it). The tax is *not* based on the value of the gift when it was first purchased. To discover the fair market value, you may need to get an appraisal or do research into book values.

Gift-Tax Filing

The gift-tax return is filed on April 15 of the year following the one in which you gave the gift. You do not have to pay the tax itself at that time; all you have to do is file the return. You can defer the gift tax and pay it later on, up to the time your estate tax is paid. For gifts between spouses, no filing is necessary, since such gifts have an unlimited exemption. And if you are under the amount of unified gift and estate-tax credit (see page 18) and have not used gift-splitting (where husband and wife give $20,000 jointly), no filing is necessary. When you do pay, the gift-tax rate will be identical to the estate-tax rate.

Many states, including California, Colorado, Delaware, Louisiana, Minnesota, New York, North Carolina, Oklahoma, Oregon, Rhode Island, South Carolina, Tennessee, Vermont, Virginia, Washington, and Wisconsin, as well as Puerto Rico, impose additional state gift taxes as well.

Gifts to a Trust

Today, each of us is entitled to a $10,000 exclusion from gift-tax payments for every beneficiary we choose, every single year. Theoretically, you have an unlimited ability to give away $10,000 every year to everyone you know. But if you make an irrevocable trust with a child or grandchild as the beneficiary and you transfer $10,000 to that trust, you cannot give that child or grandchild a separate $10,000 gift outside that trust in any one calendar year. You can, however, give them that new $10,000 gift the following calendar year. You can also give the $10,000 gift to the child's siblings, children, spouse, and anyone else you choose. You are entitled to these $10,000 and $20,000 gift-tax exclusions in addition to your lifetime $600,000 exclusion.

Changes from the Hill

What I have just described is the gift-tax situation today. Let's take a look at the gift-tax situation tomorrow.

Some senators and representatives would like to make a radical change in the gift tax. The change may be rolling back the exclusion to $3,000 a year per beneficiary, or it may be no change whatsoever. The most likely change—and this is the scuttlebutt from Washington as this book goes to press—is that the exclusion will remain at $10,000, but you will be able to give that $10,000 to only three loved ones in any given year. Those of you blessed enough to have many children or grandchildren may find yourselves giving gifts each year to different grandchildren, since three beneficiaries may be your yearly limit.

Advancements

I can give you one hint at this time: Let's say you have four, five, or six grandchildren. If the law does change, and you can only give to three beneficiaries each year, you may be concerned that in one year you will fall ill and have no opportunity to give the gift to the grandchildren you left out the year before. Taking care of this worry is really very simple. Change your will, adding what is called an *advancement clause.* This clause says that the children who have already received their $10,000 gift have gotten an advancement on their inheritance. The ones left out will get an extra $10,000, to equalize the gifts that they are getting from you.

ESTATE TAX

Perhaps the single most important purpose of gift-giving is to reduce estate taxes on a child's inheritance. Estates of over $600,000 are subject to a federal estate tax and, in most states, a state estate tax. In New York State, for example, the combined federal and state tax can come to as much as eighty-two cents on every dollar. The federal estate tax, which applies no matter in which state you reside, begins at 37 percent of the first taxable dollar and increases to as much as 55 percent.

People give gifts to reduce the amount of their *gross estate* and thereby reduce their taxes. Your gross estate includes every asset over which you can exercise control at your death. That is, if you transfer an asset but retain substantial power over it, including the right to revoke the transfer, it will still be included as part of your gross estate. Let's say you've placed an insurance policy in the name of your spouse or child. If you have reserved for yourself the right to reinvest the dividends, borrow against the policy, or change the beneficiary, the death benefit will be taxed to your estate, as the insurance policy will be considered part of your gross estate.

Trust law (see Chapter 5) is largely concerned with exempting assets from estate taxes through gifts to the trust while permitting you to retain the maximum control allowed by law.

Gift Taxes Versus Estate Taxes

A final consideration is that the estate- and gift-tax tables are *unified*. This means that whenever you give a gift that exceeds $10,000 per beneficiary per year ($20,000 for a married couple), you use up part of your $600,000 lifetime gift-tax exclusion. But very often it is wise to give a taxable gift in your lifetime rather than pass it on through an inheritance. There are two main reasons why.

First, gift-giving, unlike bequeathing, puts the growth value of the gift outside of your estate. If you gift a stock with a value of $50,000, the gift tax is imposed on only $50,000. But if you do not gift the stock and it grows in value to $70,000 by the date of death, then, as part of the inheritance, $70,000 is taxed. For this reason, professionals often call gift-giving "freezing the value of an estate."

Second, if you give a gift and pay a tax immediately, the amount of the tax is itself spent and therefore out of the estate and is not counted in the gross estate.

CAPITAL GAINS TAX

Under some circumstances you should *not* gift an already-appreciated property during your lifetime. In those cases the capital gains tax that results would be greater than the estate tax that you save. This is due to the *stepped-up basis* of valuing a security.

The Stepped-Up Basis

As of this writing, the *stepped-up basis* is still a boon to taxpayers. Basis is simply the difference between the price you paid (plus any expenses to buy, sell, or repair) and the sale price—it could be jewels, art, real estate, stocks, mutual funds, or what have you. Let's say you give the property to your child or grandchild while you are alive. The recipient is deemed to have paid the same amount for the property that you did originally. The recipient receives your original lower basis along with the gift—if he sells it, either before or after your death, he will pay a capital gains tax on the difference between *what you paid when you acquired the asset* and the price at which he sold it.

If, on the other hand, you don't give him a gift during your lifetime but instead leave him that same appreciated property in an inheritance, the recipient will be deemed to have "purchased" the property at its date-of-death value (or at its value six months later, depending on what the executor chooses. Whichever date is chosen has to apply to all assets.) This gives you a "stepped-up basis," a higher basis (and therefore a *lower* profit for tax purposes). If you have a low-basis investment, you should consider *not* giving a gift during your lifetime but creating an inheritance instead. If you make a gift during your lifetime, you must weigh the benefits of saving estate taxes (which won't come into play for most couples until they have over $1,200,000, or for most individuals until they have over $600,000) against the amount of capital gains taxes you're costing your family. Preserving the stepped-up basis can create more family wealth than saving estate taxes, depending on the circumstances.

If you're investing for your children or grandchildren through an annuity, even if the money does not pass until death, there is no *stepped-up basis* because the accumulated wealth is not considered capital gains. It is considered income, and an income tax has to be paid. And estate tax is imposed on the entire value of the annuity. So using annuities may not be the very best way to create an inheritance for your children, because you are wiping away the possibility of getting a *stepped-up* basis on the appreciation, since the appreciation is considered income, not a capital gain.

A FINAL NOTE OF CAUTION

A gift is an actual transfer of property from your possession to the possession and ownership of another (in this case, your children). The key words in this definition are *actual transfer*. A true gift must be given with all control relinquished. But many parents believe that they can put a gift on an elastic string, giving it to the child and then snatching it back when they "need the money." They set up trusts and lend money to their children without relinquishing full control over the money.

In fact, this elastic-string attitude can be detrimental to relationships. If the child is old enough to be aware that the gift is being given and taken away, it can cause psychological problems. But it can also create legal problems. The government will allow you the various tax breaks that come with gift-giving only when you divest yourself of the elastic string altogether. Examples of gifts with strings attached are gifts that are forfeited if one does not pursue a certain course of study, marry at a certain age or within a certain faith, or live within a certain radius of the family.

It is essential to keep in mind that a gift, once given, belongs to the person who receives the it (the donee), not to the person who gave it (the donor). Legal title has passed. It is for this very reason that taxes are saved in gift-giving.

Gift-giving, as we discuss it in this book, is a purely financial and tax-saving device. It can save estate taxes when individuals divest themselves of their assets. These divested assets are not counted in the estate, and therefore no estate tax is paid. Similarly, gift-giving can save income taxes since money accumulated as interest, dividends, or other income from principal given as a gift belongs to the donee. The interest, dividends, and so forth, are reported on the donee's income tax return, presumably at a lower tax rate and perhaps at a lower tax bracket than they would be for the donor.

Once you have given a gift, it is out of your control. When we discuss the many ways of giving gifts, you will see that some dominion may continue, but for the most part your power over the gifted funds is very limited.

·3·

Titling Accounts: The Joint Account

The most popular method of titling accounts, despite efforts by most well-informed trust and estate lawyers to quash the trend, is the joint account, be it an account in a bank or in stocks, in U.S. bonds, or in real estate. Parents who would like to avoid probate know that, if they put their money in an account in their own name jointly with those of their children or grandchildren, upon their death this joint account will supersede a will, avoid probate, and go directly to the children. Some people believe that they are also saving taxes. While both parties are still alive, in most joint accounts either party can sign checks and approve withdrawals and securities transactions. It seems the perfect way to give the money yet keep control.

Yet many of these supposed advantages are wrong. Here

is the truth about some of the more popular misconceptions about joint accounts:

- They do not save taxes. Truth: The tax is attributed to the Social Security number on the account. The first party to die will have the account counted in their estate.
- One party can "clean out" the account if one of the parties dies and not pay an estate tax. Truth: The bank will require a waiver showing that taxes were paid before the survivor can get the money. If they don't know about the death and the "cleaning out" party fails to disclose, that's tax evasion.
- When the parent dies, the child will inherit the money without probate. Truth: It's true, there is no probate, but imagine a scenario that begins this way: "Jane has just inherited $110,000. The trouble is, she doesn't know where the money is. Her mother never told her."

By making joint accounts in order to avoid making a will and to avoid probate, parents may be jeopardizing their money. Money in a joint account is not protected from the creditors or spouse of the joint owner. If the joint owners are husband and wife, the asset goes without probate to the survivor, but if the owners are grandparents and child or grandchild, or parent and child, there often can be friction from those left out; other grandchildren or siblings may resent it when an older person puts money in an account in the name of only one child or grandchild. Often the left-out children will try to set aside such joint designations as being the result of undue duress. By contrast, a will or trust provision is much more difficult to set aside because of the presumption of competency when the will or trust was made. But you need only observe a grandmother opening a bank account to realize the confusion involved in the task of titling an account; titling a joint account is even more complicated. So let's look at different types of joint accounts.

Some of us create joint accounts without realizing we are making permanent gifts at all. Here are a few examples:

1. *A joint bank account opened in your name and a child's (or other's) name.* A gift is considered to have been made (and a gift-tax incurred) when the other party withdraws money. No tax is incurred if each party contributed an equal amount.
2. *Purchasing a U.S. savings bond in two names.* The purchaser may cash in the bond tax-free; the other party would pay a gift tax upon cashing in the bond.
3. *Purchasing joint stock.* Naming a joint owner establishes that a gift has been made.
4. *Putting real estate in another person's name.* A gift is considered to have been made when the new deed is issued.

One problem with joint accounts is that when a parent and child are joint owners and one of them dies, the amount of holdings added to the decedent's estate is determined by who purchased and contributed to the holdings. It may thus be possible for all the holdings to be considered part of the estate of the first to die.

Another problem occurs if there is a simultaneous death. Then there are no instructions at all. It can happen that a child or grandchild dies either before the older person or at the time the older person becomes incompetent to handle the money. If that happens, no new beneficiary can be designated by the parent or grandparent. Instead, the court will take over.

And finally, the creditors of both parties can take money from a joint account.

With no tax savings and the potential for so much mischief, I never recommend joint accounts. If you are giving a gift through a joint account solely to avoid probate, you are much better off with a revocable trust. If you don't want one, I suggest you make a simple will and not try to avoid probate at all.

Joint accounts have several variations in their titling. One kind is called the POD, or payable on death account. An in trust for (ITF) account, sometimes called a Totten trust, is also often used when no present gift is intended but when probate is intended to be avoided. While these accounts do supersede a will, their very ambiguity creates a problem. What happens if the giver withdraws money and transfers it to a new POD? What happens if the ITF account was set up years ago, but there is a recent will? The answers to these questions are fought out in surrogate courts every day.

POTENTIAL TAX PROBLEMS

For all types of "will substitute" or probate-avoiding accounts: Be aware of potential tax problems.

When someone opens up an account in his own name together with that of a minor, he creates a joint account. But confusion arises as to the proper method of taxing such an account. At least one tax court has held that interest earned on joint accounts is taxable to the owners in proportion to their contributions. Another court held that the contributions were immaterial and that taxes were to be assessed on an equal basis. For the most part, the government will view joint accounts as remaining in the control of the adult. A true custodial account can thus have legal ramifications.

Caution: An important point to consider is the use of Social Security numbers in opening up joint accounts. Frequently, a lower-tax-paying grandmother will, without informing her children or grandchildren, set up a joint account. The interest from that account is money that she expects to declare and pay taxes on at her lower tax bracket. If the Social Security number of the child is listed first, however, the government may consider that the funds belong to the child, precipitating an audit against an often unsuspecting child. To avoid this, be careful to list only the Social Security number of the person with the lower tax bracket or to list this number first.

Finally, here is my round-up of the joint account's negative features, even if probate is avoided.

1. An executor of a will can choose to attack the designation if it is in conflict with an existing will.
2. In the event that the beneficiary dies first, there is no planning. The parent must redesignate a beneficiary, but they may be incompetent or forget to do so.
3. In the event of a simultaneous death, state law will apply. No taxes will be saved. And there is no protection for you—mother, father, grandmother, or grandfather—in the event of your incompetency, unless you have also made a power of attorney.

In short, the methods to avoid probate do work, but can backfire if not carefully considered. I realize that in discouraging the creation of joint accounts, I may lose some credibility because I earn a living drafting trusts and wills. (Or at least I used to before I got involved in writing and media.) But truthfully, trust and estate attorneys make more money handling estate battles than drafting wills.

If your purpose in titling accounts jointly is to avoid probate, don't do it. Keep the money in your own name, and make a simple will or revocable trust. If your purpose is convenience, don't do it, either. Make a power of attorney instead. (See Chapter 10.) If you think you will save taxes, you won't. Enough said!

·4·

Titling Accounts:
The Uniform Gifts to Minors Act

THE UNIFORM GIFTS TO MINORS ACT

The Uniform Gifts to Minors Act (UGMA) has been adopted by every state. It governs the giving of money, securities, life insurance policies, or annuities to anyone under twenty-one. A custodian must be appointed to manage these gifts for the minor. Any adult family member, guardian, lawyer, or trust company may be appointed a custodian. If a professional is appointed a custodian, a fee is paid; if a family member becomes a custodian, there is no fee paid. If the gift is of money, life insurance policies, annuities, or registered securities, the donor of the gift may be appointed custodian. If unregistered securities are given, the donor may not be appointed custodian.

The custodian is empowered to manage, hold, and invest

the property of the minor. He may sell or exchange this property, the proceeds to be used for the minor's benefit. The custodian must also keep careful records, register all securities, and establish a bank account for the money. In short, the custodian assumes all fiduciary responsibility for the property. The minor receives the money upon reaching the age of twenty-one. If the minor should die before age twenty-one, the money becomes part of the minor's gross estate.

If Aunt Sally sets up an account with a mutual fund under UGMA, she remains custodian of the funds. She can buy, sell, or add to them. If the minor who is the beneficiary of the account dies, then the assets are counted in his estate. In the more likely event that the minor lives to be twenty-one he will receive the money outright, no strings attached.

The custodial gift is irrevocable; it belongs to the minor. Although the custodian (or donor) is empowered to control and manage the money, any tax due from earned income is taxed according to the rate for the trust and not for the custodian's personal income. If the donor dies before the minor reaches twenty-one, however, the property will accrue to the donor's estate, and estate tax will have to be paid.

These custodial accounts are the modern replacement for court-ordered legal guardianship over money. A custodial account really does transfer the asset and give the gift to the child; yet the gift-giver or other custodian handles the money.

TYPES OF CUSTODIAL ACCOUNTS

There are two types of custodial accounts. The UGMA—the Uniform Gifts to Minors Account—and the UTMA—the Uniform Transfers to Minors Account—are actually very similar. The main difference between them is in the type of property that you are permitted to transfer to your child. UGMAs permit transfers only of bank deposits, securities (such as mutual funds), and insurance policies. But in states with UTMA regulations, you can transfer any kind of property to the account. You should find out if your state has UTMA regulations, which supersede UGMA regulations.

Both types of accounts allow you to set money aside on behalf of a minor and control the assets of that account until the child reaches the age of *majority* in your state, usually eighteen or twenty-one.

To establish a custodial account, you'll need to get a Social Security number for the child. You can apply for one at the hospital where your child was born or through the Social Security Administration.

TAX-WISE PLANNING

The kiddie tax applies to money earned in a UGMA or a UTMA. (See Chapter 2.) Refresh your memory about the tax with this chart:

Child under 14
- The first $650 of income is tax-free.
- Income of $651 to $1,300 is taxed at 15 percent.
- Income over $1,300 is taxed at the parents' rate.

Child 14 or over
- All income over $1,200 is taxed at the child's rate (assuming the child's income is filed with the parents' tax return).

PROS AND CONS OF CUSTODIAL ACCOUNTS

Under the law of every state, once you transfer funds to a custodial account, the gift belongs to the child immediately, even though the child needs a custodian to manage the gift.

One advantage of these accounts is that the income from the funds is taxed at the minor's rate. If the child is over fourteen, he is in his own, presumably lower tax bracket: lower than yours, and lower than his parents'. So a Uniform Gifts to Minors Act or a Uniform Transfers to Minors Act gift can work very well taxwise for children over fourteen.

Another plus is that the custodian controls the use of the money without any court intervention until the child comes of age. This age can be anywhere from eighteen to twenty-one, depending on state law. At that time the money comes under the child's control. Up until the age of majority, however, the custodian controls the funds. If you are a grandma or grandpa, you can appoint your children as custodians. Then they have the fiduciary duties and obligations with respect to the child and the money. The custodial account is a fine idea if you want to transfer your assets now.

Another advantage: The funds and all their growth avoid probate. Since the money is out of your estate, it also avoids estate taxes on its growth from the day you set up the custodial account.

On the negative side, the UGMA and UTMA accounts are irrevocable. The money is no longer yours, and you can never get it back. It is the child's, with no strings attached.

Also, if you act as custodian, you can invest the money only in certain types of simple securities, like CDs and other clearly investment-grade securities.

If you want the children to have control over those assets as soon as they reach the age of majority, and if you want to transfer the taxation to a child fourteen years old or older, such an account is a good idea. But it is not a good idea if you think you will want the money back, if you may need that money in the future. It cannot be used for any family purpose, only for the purpose of the child.

A custodial account may also be a poor idea if the child would otherwise have a chance to get college aid. (See Chapter 11.)

Finally, Unified Gifts to Minors and Unified Transfers to Minors accounts are free, and they are very easy to set up. So if you do want to use them, you will not need an attorney. You can simply use your broker or banker.

·5·

Trusts

A trust is a fundamental tool for tax planning. It can transfer an appreciating asset to a beneficiary and still allow the grantor (gift giver) to name a trustee and to institute controls over the assets. Once transferred to the trust, the asset is no longer part of the estate of the gift giver, nor is the future appreciation of the asset. Income-producing assets may not be the best assets to transfer, because the tax legislation has actually increased the income taxation of trusts above that of individuals. Therefore, while raw land, stocks, and tangibles are excellent trust assets, bonds and income-producing real estate may not be.

Trusts are wonderful tools created especially to save taxes while permitting the gift-giver to maintain a degree of control over the gift. At one time, trusts were largely for the very wealthy, since they were the group most stung by the tax bite. But that's no longer so today.

Middle-class families are relying both on trusts and on a new device called the family limited partnership to protect their wealth. The purpose is not only to save taxes, but to protect family assets from creditors in our overly litigious society and to monitor gifts so that marital disputes and other issues don't get in the way of wealth transfer. Trusts also aid in the avoidance of costly probate and in the management of money.

WHAT IS A TRUST?

A trust is defined by the Internal Revenue Code Regulations as "an arrangement created either by will or by an inter vivos [during your lifetime] declaration whereby trustees take title to property for the purpose of protecting or conserving it for the beneficiaries under the ordinary rules applied in chancery or probate court."

In English, this means that a trust is a written document by which one person or corporation, called a *grantor,* gives money to a second person or corporation, called a *trustee,* to hold for the benefit of a third person, called the *beneficiary.* At termination of the trust, its assets are given over to the beneficiary of the principal, called the *remainderman.* There are many kinds of trusts, but all are fundamentally structured this way.

The rules of each state apply to the administration and validity of a trust. But a trust created and valid in one state is valid in every state. Thus, grandparents who create trusts before they move to a retirement residence in a new state are assured that the trust is valid.

HOW TRUSTS BUILD WEALTH

Lower Tax Bracket

A trust creates a new taxpayer: the trust itself. Under some circumstances the trust itself pays taxes to the government. That is, the trust itself is taxed for the money it earns, not the grantor or the beneficiary. When does a trust file its own return? Answer: When the grantor retains little or no control over the use of the trust. The grantor relinquishes control by naming another person the trustee and by keeping for him- or herself only limited power over the funds. This kind of trust is called an *irrevocable trust,* and it gets its own tax identification number and files its own separate tax return through its trustee. It contrasts with the *revocable trust,* which is reported on the tax return of the grantor.

Whether a trust is revocable or irrevocable is irrelevant to the IRS. Logic dictates. If the grantor can use the trust fund in any way he or she wishes, the government views the trust as merely a sham, a device to create a taxpayer in a lower tax bracket than the grantor.

Do You Want the Trust Rate to Apply?

Ever since the Omnibus Budget Reconciliation Act of 1993, the usefulness of irrevocable trusts for tax saving has come into question. Take one look at the new tax brackets created by the act and you will see why:

Tax on Trusts
15% on taxable income under $1,500
28% on taxable income over $1,500 but under $3,500
31% of taxable income over $3,500 but under $5,500

36% of taxable income over $5,500 but under $7,500
39.6% of taxable income over $7,500

By comparison, without a trust the 36 percent tax rate applies to married couples only if they have taxable income of more than $140,000, while the top 39.6 percent rate applies to those earning over $250,000. The income tax rate for trust income, in other words, is far steeper than the income tax rate for the parent or child. But, as we will see, very effective planning can keep the tax down and the other benefits of trusts intact.

The 1993 act increased the number of tax brackets under which irrevocable trusts must file, so that giving even a few dollars to children can result in taxation in a higher bracket. Before you make any new gifts, even if you have an existing irrevocable trust, check with your accountant. Keep in mind, however, that these trusts do save you inheritance tax or estate tax, because they do divest you of assets that are then not counted in your estate.

When Are Trust Assets Taxed at the Beneficiary's Bracket?

Trust income may be taxed at the rate and bracket of the income beneficiary if the beneficiary actually receives the income. If a trust fund earns interest or dividends or increases in other ways and the trustee distributes this income to the beneficiary, the beneficiary is taxed on that income. If the income accumulates in the trust fund, on the other hand, the trust pays the income tax. If the trust fund is made up of tax-free securities, the income beneficiary, of course, pays no tax.

In sum: If funds are accumulated in the trust, the tax bracket and tax rate that apply to the trust are those that apply to the income derived from the investment of the funds. If income is distributed to the child beneficiary, then the child's tax bracket and rate apply to the income derived from those funds. In either case, if the trust or the child beneficiary is in a lower tax bracket than the parent-grantor, setting up a trust will reduce taxes and increase wealth.

Types of Trusts Compared

An inter vivos trust (the Latin literally means "between living persons") is a trust that you create during your lifetime. You can be both the grantor and the trustee. The trust can terminate on your death or during your own lifetime. An inter vivos trust can pour over into another trust in your will, so that it continues even after your death.

A testamentary trust, by contrast, is a trust created only in your will, and comes into action only upon your death. It is part of your Last Will and Testament. If you change your will, you can eliminate it. (If you already have an inter vivos trust, you can instruct in your will what to do with it. If your instructions are to take inter vivos trust funds and "pour" them into a testamentary trust fund, this is called a "pour-over" provision.)

Here is a comparison of how the two different kinds of trusts help build wealth:

Inter Vivos Trust

- Takes effect during your lifetime.
- Can save on estate taxes.
- Allows you to see how your fiduciaries control and use the funds.
- Gives property away irrevocably if estate taxes are to be saved.

- Can be revocable, but if it is, no estate taxes will be saved.
- Can save on income taxes because they will be paid either at the trust's rate or at the beneficiary's rate.

Testamentary Trust

- Takes effect at your death.
- Controls the use of money even after your death.
- Allows for long-range tax planning.
- Retains property during your lifetime.
- Taxes your property along with the rest of your estate.
- Has no income tax advantage.

Protecting "Untouchable" Money

A parent who considers certain funds "untouchable" and sets them aside, say, for the children's education, is likely to draw upon those funds anyway in a crisis. That is, the funds were only *mentally* set aside; they were not *legally* set aside. Placing the same funds in trust, however, sets up a legal barrier to using them, allowing wealth to be built. It is true that the trust may provide for an invasion of principal, but the parent will be more reluctant to use that money because of the income tax penalty for doing so. Remember, if the grantor uses money for his or her own use or even to support the minor child beneficiary, it will be considered the grantor's money.

Professional Management

Trusts also help build wealth by encouraging professional management and continuity of management. By either naming a professional as the trustee or using a professional to help build wealth, you are focusing and directing the professional to a special purpose. Financial planners do their best job if they know how much you wish to invest and for what purpose.

Continuity in a Crisis

A rather odd way that trusts help build wealth is through the avoidance of intrafamily squabbles. The trust continues to be administered as you directed. Funds are invested and income is distributed to the beneficiary of your choice, even during the period of contest. By contrast, if a will is contested in probate, the proceedings are prolonged. Money remains in the estate without being managed except, perhaps, by the executor during the contest, which may take many years.

Capital Gains Tax Savings

A trust can also be useful to diminish that species of income tax called the capital gains tax. For example: Let's say you purchased some property at a low price, and through the years that property has appreciated greatly and is continuing to appreciate. By transferring this rapidly appreciating property to a trust, the increased value of this property is not counted in your estate. This aspect is particularly useful for grandparents, who may not need to liquidate and sell their property during their lifetime but are planning to give their property to their grandchildren. Always check with your accountant to see if you would be better off leaving the property in a will to take advantage of the stepped-up basis. (See pages 18–20.)

Estate Tax Savings

If you create a trust that is irrevocable, estate taxes will be saved. This is because Uncle Sam counts as part of your gross estate only those assets over which you have control at the time of your death. By relinquishing control over assets to an irrevocable trust during your lifetime, you have actually divested yourself of the use, possession, and control of those assets. Therefore, it is only fair—and Uncle Sam thinks so, too—to eliminate the trust funds from your gross estate in determining your estate taxes.

Gift Tax

It should also be noted that you pay a gift tax when you transfer money to a trust. If the amount of the transfer is less than the gift tax exclusion ($10,000 per person per year or $20,000 per married couple per year), then you pay no tax.

Each beneficiary of a trust can get $10,000 excluded from tax. *Caveat:* If you have given an outright gift in a certain year to a beneficiary, you cannot double-dip by making that person the beneficiary of a trust, too, in the same year. The fact that the person is receiving a gift through a trust does not matter; the $10,000 exclusion is used up by your outright gift.

HOW TO SET UP A TRUST

There are many variables in setting up a trust. For example, the income beneficiary (the one who gets the income earned by the trust fund) and the remainderman (the one who gets the trust fund itself when the trust terminates) can be the same person. The grantor (the person who transfers the money in the first place) can also be the trustee (the person who handles, invests, and distributes the money). The duration, purpose, and amount of money or the type of assets placed in a trust can vary. Trusts are governed by state law, and states have different requirements for setting them up and different interpretations of the language of trusts. Theoretically, a trust with any type of grantor/trustee/beneficiary combination can be set up for any legal purpose.

If you are convinced that a trust would be useful to you, visit your attorney. If your attorney is an expert in estate planning, he or she will develop with you the kind of trust that you need to meet your goals. In our offices we begin with the goal itself, then take the client through a checklist of needs that are on his or her personal horizon. Once the goals have been articulated, drafting the trust itself is rather simple. Remember that in all areas of tax and estate planning, you give something to get something. You will be trading financial liquidity for tax savings or financial control for management potential.

Overall goals prioritized from 1 to 10 with 10 being most important

Tax savings—estate	_____
Tax savings—income	_____
Dividing assets fairly	_____
Dividing assets equally	_____
Helping my children	_____
Helping my grandchildren	_____
Giving to charity	_____
Disowning	_____
Preserving the family business	_____
Other	_____

In setting up your trusts, consider the following goals and their implementation:

1. Professional Management. Create a revocable trust that you can terminate at will for maximum flexibility. Observe the performance of a professional trustee to see whether you wish to create an irrevocable or testamentary trust. You will not save any income tax or estate taxes since you continue to exercise dominion.

2. Estate-Tax Savings. Create an irrevocable trust in which you give up control and shift the rights to the income and the principal to your child beneficiary. Upon your death this money will not be counted for estate tax purposes.

3. Capital Gains Tax Savings. Create an irrevocable trust during your lifetime in which you transfer highly appreciated property. Have that property distributed to your income beneficiary if he is in a low tax bracket. To save estate taxes on the capital appreciation, merely make the trust irrevocable, and the highly appreciated asset will not be counted in your estate.

4. Save Income Taxes. Create an irrevocable long-term or short-term trust that transfers the income to your child beneficiary and therefore taxes the investment at the child's tax bracket and rate rather than your own higher tax bracket and rate.

5. Flexibility and Invasion of Principal for Special Needs. A special trust provision called a Crummey Clause can be used, under which your beneficiary has the right to demand or withdraw approximately

$10,000 per year from the trust principal to use in the event of an emergency.

6. Annual Gift-Tax Exclusion. Money in a trust will qualify for the annual gift-tax exclusion if the income may be distributed to the minor prior to reaching age twenty-one. The payments can be limited to providing for the minor's welfare, maintenance, education, and support only. The term of the trust can be delayed so that it ends after the child is twenty-one, as long as the donee has the right to compel the distribution of the trust principal at age twenty-one.

·6·

Trust Provisions of Special Interest to Parents and Grandparents

In defining your goals and creating trusts, you should discuss with your attorney not only the financial aspects of the trust provisions but the administrative aspects as well. A lot of what you decide will depend upon the personalities of your child and yourself. Some special provisions of interest to parents are the spendthrift provision, the accumulation provision, and the Crummey provision.

THE SPENDTHRIFT PROVISION

Spendthrift provisions in trusts were created for rich people whose spoiled children were spending trust income before it was distributed to them. Creditors such as jewelry stores and automobile dealers were often willing to accept a marker giving them the right to collect future trust-guaranteed income. Some would-be heirs had all their future income pledged to creditors.

A spendthrift provision protects these people from themselves. It doesn't give them any interest on the income until it is distributed, so that they can't give it away beforehand. Such provisions can also empower the trustee to make only direct payments to a doctor or a school on behalf of the beneficiary instead of giving them income.

THE ACCUMULATION PROVISION

Accumulation provisions in trusts can be set up with no income paid to the beneficiary. Instead, the money is accumulated in the trust. The money earned by the trust is taxed every year at the tax rate set for the trust's own tax bracket. When it is finally paid out to the beneficiary, a special tax is imposed at the beneficiary's bracket, as if the income had been paid to him or her in the years it was being earned. The taxes the trust itself has paid now come back to the beneficiary as a credit against the new taxes. (This is called throwback.) Meanwhile, the extra tax the beneficiary would have had to pay through the years has been invested elsewhere. Better yet, if the income was accumulated before the beneficiary reached the age of twenty-one, only the tax the trust paid is imposed. If the money is paid out after the child turns twenty-one, the tax may be slightly higher; the added tax is the difference between the amount the trust has actually paid and the amount the beneficiary would have had to pay after age twenty-one, had the trust income been paid to him.

THE CRUMMEY PROVISION

Crummey is the name of one of the more famous cases in trusts and estate history. It permits a beneficiary to demand up to $10,000 a year from a trust, which is then considered the same as your giving a gift of that amount. Such a gift is completely tax-free. It is not included as income to the gift-getter, nor is it included in determining a gift tax or estate tax for the gift-giver. In making a trust with a Crummey provision, you are actually creating another donor who is entitled to give $10,000 a year tax-free. This newly created donor is the trust itself.

To take advantage of Crummey, the beneficiary need only demand the $10,000. However, there are some simple limits to these Crummey provisions:

- The beneficiary can demand the $10,000 only once in any given calendar year. If he permits the year to go by without demanding the money, that year is up and the money can no longer be paid.
- The beneficiary will get the money only if a transfer is made to the trust itself.
- The beneficiary must receive notice of the right to withdraw and a reasonable opportunity to exercise the right.

In case your beneficiary does not call for the $10,000 gift and lets it lapse, the Internal Revenue Service considers this a gift by your beneficiary to the trust. By not accepting a gift and merely leaving the money there your beneficiary has augmented the amount in the trust.

But the IRS does permit a beneficiary to leave up to $5,000 or 5 percent of the amount of the corpus (funds) in the trust (whichever is larger) without being subject to a gift tax. This is a great lesson in the workings of the IRS. It shows you how much the Service, as it is informally known, loves to create problems and then find ways to solve them.

·7·

Selecting Trustees

Parents have a natural tendency to wish to be the trustee for the trust they establish. Their desire to control funds and to save trustee fees is normal. Psychologically, they may not really feel that the money used to fund the trust belongs to the minor. Instead, they see the money as theirs and the trust as only a tax device. By naming another person as trustee, they may feel that they are getting too close to relinquishing their rights over the money. These feelings may block actually setting up a trust.

As we have already seen, naming the parent or grandparent as trustee may interfere with tax-saving strategies. In other cases, such as grantor trusts, an outside trustee can be named, but certain rights over the funds are reserved for the grantor. If estate-tax saving is a primary goal, however, grantor control must be very limited.

For these reasons, most parents and grandparents with

taxable estates need to appoint an outside trustee. The rules of choosing such a trustee are largely a matter of common sense.

Many people consider their brother-in-law or a friend who is smart in business as the possible trustee of either an inter vivos or a testamentary trust. Often the problem of choosing a trustee brings about family tensions. It is also common for male chauvinism to crop up. Frequently, a husband who has accumulated the family wealth and who has made a will leaving substantial amounts to his wife thinks that she is incapable of handling the estate. The result is that sometimes an incompetent male relative is appointed instead of the wife, who is given no right in the will to get rid of him and suffers as a consequence.

On the other hand, not every spouse, male or female, would make a good trustee. You may ask your spouse to be a trustee, but only you know what will give you peace of mind. It generally does not work to appoint other relatives as trustees. No one likes to be at the mercy of a family member. People are reluctant to give information to their in-laws, or worse, their in-laws' spouses. It is often better to work with paid professionals, at least one—maybe even two—no matter how conservative they are. I often suggest co-fiduciaries—one of them the major beneficiary, such as your spouse, the other a paid professional.

The next question is inevitable: Whom should I use as a paid professional—an institution or an individual? Believe it or not, it may be wise to use both. An institution has the double advantage of continuity and personnel. It may have a large team of experts, so that should one expert leave or die, someone will be there to take over immediately.

The individual, meanwhile, has the advantage of offering service, understanding, and intimacy. An individual lawyer who knows the family and is sensitive as well as knowledgeable can single-handedly make the investment suggestions best suited to individual cases. Remember that large institutions do not plan investments for you alone. They often have hundreds of other clients and make mass investment strategies.

The individual, by contrast, knows you personally and handles you separately. Frankly, individual experts may also be more in need of your business. They need you because you may make up one percent, instead of one-millionth of one percent, of their business.

Of course, there's a drawback: Individual trustees may discover problems they can't handle, and therefore they may have to hire other experts to help, using your money. Also, they may have no one to take the helm if they should become disabled.

Today, the practicalities of estate practice are such that no one can really handle it alone, although the client should not be burdened with multiple consultations. Estate planners often work with or are also lawyers, accountants, pension planners, ERISA* specialists.

When you talk to your planner, ask about his or her support network. Even with all the professionals involved, estate planning is a cost-effective tax-saving method. Tax savings

---

* This stands for the Employee Retirement Income Security Act, a federal statute which uniformly regulates employee benefits such as pension and health insurance and the tax consequences of benefit contributions and receipts.

can be huge, and the degree of the work is in proportion to the amount that can be saved.

Further, where warranted, it is not unusual to have two or three trustees. The main beneficiary is appointed a trustee together with an institution and an individual counselor. The individual counselor keeps up the dialogue with the institution and has equal say. The institution uses its expertise for investment.

Your individual lawyer can respond immediately, having no bureaucracy to contend with. That doesn't mean you'll get your way; it just means you'll be able to voice your opinion and, as a fiduciary, have a vote. Depending on the terms of the trust, the individual or institutional fiduciary can be outvoted.

Conflicts can always occur, even between institutions and individuals—perhaps I should say *especially* between institutions and individuals. But you can avoid this by getting them together early on. Even if your trust is made in your will—testamentary—have them meet, both with and without you. Often enough, my clients have sent me to lunch with a bank manager or trust officer of the institution they have chosen. That's very wise: As we know each other, we work better together. If something happens to the institutional fiduciary, I have been there all along and can educate whoever takes over. If something happened to me, the institution's professional would be there to educate my successor. Institutions are made up of highly professional people, and the individual you choose must be a knowledgeable and reliable person.

Using a co-trustee may be just the way to keep a widow or widower in touch with the money that is rightfully theirs and still have them work side by side with a professional. He or she should also have the right to fire the professional if the work is not being done properly, as long as another one is appointed immediately. But it must be remembered that co-trustees are equal fiduciaries. Your spouse may feel small and unimportant next to the big, powerful corporation that is co-trustee. This can sometimes lead to nonparticipation. In turn, the corporate trustee may take over, and make investment decisions without consultation.

The solution to this dilemma is to prepare your beneficiary. One good way is to have him or her read this book. To help co-fiduciaries further along, have an emergency clause for illness or disability; a delegation clause for temporary absence; and a hold-harmless clause if one trustee (like the shy spouse) doesn't participate. There can even be a difference-of-opinion clause in case of an impasse. Majority rule is a possibility, or something like this:

> In the event of a difference of opinion, the (corporate or individual) trustee's decision shall apply, provided it is given in writing to the other. The (individual or corporate) trustee shall abide by the decision of the other and shall not be liable for the actions of the trustees made pursuant to the decision.

Use the individual as a special trustee with review powers for sprinkling (distributing money at various times and in differing amounts to beneficiaries), accumulation, or invasion. For example, an attorney can be named as trustee for the sole purpose of determining whether income should be accumulated or distributed between beneficiaries, or even whether the principal should be invaded. An institution can have investment control. Be flexible and creative. Most things can be done. Just remember that in judging fiduciaries the criteria are:

1. Continuity. Will they be around long enough that no one else will have to choose the fiduciary after you're gone?
2. Consistency. Is this an institution that changes personnel all the time, or is the individual one who will pass you off to subordinates?
3. Conversation. Is there a dialogue among you, your beneficiary, and your fiduciary—a willingness to talk?
4. Calculation. How have they done in the past with other people's money? (They will be able to give you some idea of this without breaching the confidentiality of their other clients.)

Once you decide on using a bank or another institution as your fiduciary, you will have to take the next step and decide which bank to choose. Most of us are ill equipped to judge institutions. But, when I interviewed Rosie James, trust officer at the former Bankers Trust, and Maureen Bateman, one of Bankers Trust's attorneys, both of them insisted that good judgment and common sense go a long way toward helping you find the right people for the job.

How do you judge a bank? You start with the people. How will the bank assign personnel to your account? The best institutions try to match customers to account executives and trust officers. Ideally, customers with similar needs will be served by the same person, who has expertise in the needed area. Ask about the procedure for switching within the bank if you're not satisfied. Don't be shy about this; it can and does happen.

Talk to the people at the bank or other institution and have your spouse speak with them too. Watch what kind of advertising and public outreach it is doing. Like lawyers, institutions try to create an image that they want to project. Banks are not shy about disclosing the kind of business they want. It's up to you to express the kind of service you want.

Also compare the investment policies at various banks and institutions. For example, do they use their own common funds as the vehicle for investing money in a trust for which they have been named as trustee? Ask for three to five years' worth of performance records. Compare these with the performance records of other common funds. Use the following indicators, which can be found in your newspaper, for comparison: the Dow Jones industrial average, Standard & Poor's composite index, and the New York Stock Exchange index. Also ask what type of fund is being used: Is it one that emphasizes income, growth, or tax-free returns?

Also compare the institutions' requirements for acceptance of becoming a fiduciary. Most institutions will not take on a trust or act as trustee unless there is a certain amount of money in the trust. Some banks actively seek individual trust accounts and are flexible. They may take on a smaller trust if it is not complex and if it fits in easily with the kind of management they are used to.

See how institutions act toward your individual co-trustees. For the most part, they will insist on being paid as much as they would be if they were sole trustees. There are few variations in this, but you might shop around. Even more important, however, is the relationship between the family member, or individual lawyer, named as trustee, and the bank. See how well they communicate with each other. This is particularly important if you have special assets to manage, like copyrights and royalties.

If you are considering a bank and simply want to test the water, you have two ways of doing this before you name a permanent trustee:

1. You can open an advisory account. The account is totally in your control, and no trust is set up. But the bank does give investment advice and handles your investments. It will charge you slightly more than it would for acting as trustee, because it is not limited by statute. In states without statutory limitations, the charges may be the same. But it is the investment advice in which you are interested. Familiarizing yourself with a bank's investment performance can be very important.
2. Set up a revocable trust. This is one way to judge the performance of any trustee.

Finally, no trustee worth its salt will prevent you from including a discharge clause in your trust document. Just as you might want to change the trustee, it is also possible the trustee will wish to renounce their role during the course of the trust. Usually, however, if a trustee does not want to serve, they will simply disqualify themselves at the time the inter vivos trust is created or the will is probated. Either eventuality gives another good reason to make sure you have good substitute trustees lined up.

A few words now about costs. The expense of multiple trustees is not necessarily forbidding. Some states don't permit lawyers to double-charge: They can't charge legal fees and fiduciary fees both. Usually the legal fees are greater and prevail.

Some states provide statutory limits for charges by fiduciaries based upon the amount of principal in a trust each year. New York provides that three trustees must share the fee of two trustees if the trust is valued at $100,000 to $200,000. If the trust is valued at more than $200,000, each trustee is entitled to one full statutory commission—unless there are more than three, in which case a total of three commissions is apportioned. Most fees are on a sliding scale of *up to* 5 percent of the amount of the trust per year for trusts of $100,000 or less and down to ½ percent for trusts of more than $2 million.

So you might pay the same amount for multiple trustees as you would if you had only one institutional fiduciary and still needed legal work. Banks and other institutions will provide rate schedules on demand, but they require yearly minimum fees for taking the account.

When you are considering institutional trustees:

1. Question them about the complexity of assets they are used to handling.
2. Pick an institution that operates in all of the localities where you have assets and beneficiaries.
3. Ask your lawyer to advise you, and encourage coordination.
4. Introduce your beneficiaries to the fiduciary and consider their response.

In deciding between family members and professionals, ask yourself whether you hold stock in a close corporation. Families whose major income comes from closely held corporations and farms should consider the paid professional executor before any other.

In general, the thing to be feared least is that your money will be mishandled. People in this field are generally honest; if anything, they are overly conservative because as a fiduciary the executor or trustee has a special legal relationship to you and to your beneficiaries. Fiduciaries must exercise prudence, good judgment, and reasonable care. If they do not, they can be accused of negligence or gross negligence. Such an accusation can mean fines, loss of reputation, replacement of money lost, or even imprisonment.

They do not have investment products to sell, nor do they take your money under management. That is left to the brokers selected by the client.

·8·

The Child's Trust

Parents in high income brackets looking to establish trusts for their children's education have long shunned UGMA and UTMA accounts in favor of trusts created under the Internal Revenue Code, Section 2503c, because they want more control over the funds. As we have seen, however, greater control can mean higher taxes, and there was always the fear that a gift tax would be imposed or that the income from the trust would be taxed at the parents' higher bracket.

Since the Omnibus Budget Reconciliation Act of 1993 raised the taxes on trusts, however, the 2503c trust has become a means of "having your cake and eating it too." It is a way of getting money out of your estate for tax purposes and still applying your tax bracket to the income earned by the trust. This can mean a big saving if your tax bracket is lower than the new trust tax brackets imposed under the act. Your accountant will advise you.

I predict that the 2503c trust will become increasingly valuable to the average family.

QUALIFYING YOUR 2503C TRUST FOR THE GIFT-TAX EXCLUSION

The so-called minor's, child's, or 2503c trust allows you to put money aside for the benefit of a child up to a maximum of age twenty-one. Under Section 2503c of the Internal Revenue Code, you will qualify for the annual $10,000 gift-tax exclusion even if you don't give a gift directly to a child or place it in a UGMA or UTMA account.

For the gift to qualify for the exclusion, however, you must follow certain rules and regulations. If you do not, you will not get your annual gift-tax exclusion. Here are the rules:

1. The law provides that the trustee may expend the trust income and principal for or on behalf of a minor beneficiary. Any amounts remaining in the trust when the beneficiary becomes twenty-one years old must be distributed to them. This provision could be a disadvantage if you would rather postpone distribution of the trust to your beneficiary until after age 21, or if you want to pay out in installments.

2. If the beneficiary, under 2503c trust, dies before reaching the age of twenty-one, the trust property must go to the beneficiary's estate, or as the beneficiary designates. If you, the gift-giver, are not the trustee or one of the trustees, the trust property is removed from the beneficiary's gross estate for federal estate-tax purposes.

3. You cannot use the funds for your own benefit or for the benefit of the household in general, or to discharge a legal obligation to your child. Many parents, and particularly grandparents, mistakenly believe that they can transfer money to the trust for their children in order to save estate taxes and still get an income stream and control the method of investing that money. Moreover, if money in a 2503c trust is used to discharge a parent's or guardian's normal legal obligation to support the minor, then the money is taxed to the parent or the guardian, not at the child's perhaps-lower tax bracket.

Let's say you want to set up an account for college and for your child's future. You transfer assets to a 2503c trust. You then discover that your school district is not as good as you thought it was, despite your horrendous real estate taxes. You decide to take your child out of public school and put him or her in a private elementary school.

Or perhaps your child becomes ill and you need extra money for the medical bills.

In most states, providing an elementary education or health care for a child is considered a legal obligation of the parent. If the parent uses trust funds to pay for these obligations, the tax bracket of the parent will apply.

To determine whether this is good or bad for you, compare your bracket with the trusts bracket for the kiddie tax. In fact, study the kiddie tax carefully. If the child is over the age of fourteen and is already in a lower tax bracket than yours, you may be actually putting the income tax burden back on yourself by using the money for various obligations that are your legal responsibility.

If you are setting up these accounts for college, and don't use them for other things, you're safe. College tuition is not a legal obligation of a parent in any state. (Under some divorce decrees, however, a divorced father or mother, by contract or by divorce order, must support a child through college.)

HAVING YOUR CAKE AND EATING IT TOO—THE IRS WAY

Because of the 1993 change in the income taxation of trusts, (see Chapter 5), many parents and grandparents are finding that while trusts save them estate taxes, they cost them income taxes. Therefore they have curtailed or abandoned their use of trusts.

Fortunately, there is a strategy that can help you have your cake and eat it too. The income from the trust can be taxed at the grantor's rate while the corpus of the trust is still kept out of the gross estate. This strategy is called the *grantor trust*. It is simply a variation of the child's trust where the grantor keeps control.

Certain rules, called the *grantor rules*, were set forth in the Internal Revenue Code to prevent grantors from using trusts to save income tax, back in the old days when trust tax brackets were more favorable than individual tax brackets. The rules prevented the grantor from holding on to too much power over the trust funds. If the rules were broken, then the income of the trust was taxed to the grantor, not the trust.

When trusts saved you income taxes, this was a terrible consequence. Today it is a desired effect because of the high tax brackets associated with trusts.

Let's learn the grantor rules so we can break them. Section 674 of the IRS Code says that if the creator of a trust or anyone else other than an adverse (remember that word *adverse*) party has the power to control the principal or the income without the consent of an adverse party, then the income is taxable to the grantor (to you, the parent).

What is an adverse party? An adverse party is anyone having a *substantial* beneficial interest in the trust who is affected by the exercise or nonexercise of power over the trust funds. For example, a beneficiary is an adverse party. A person who is not an adverse party is someone who has no beneficial interest, such as a stranger trustee, or less than a substantial beneficial interest, such as a disinterested family member.

Since in the old days (before 1993) the major goal of forming trusts for children was to save income tax, it was a failure if the parents eventually had to pay taxes at their higher level despite the trust. This situation could arise under the IRS if the grantor or someone not an adverse party had control over the money. If you named yourself or someone not an adverse party as trustee, you had control and could be in danger of having the trust income taxed at your rate.

Powers Retained by the Grantor

A grantor can keep certain powers regardless of whether he or she is named as trustee, and the trust's bracket and rate will still apply. The retainable powers include: withholding income during the disability of a beneficiary; distributing principal to the beneficiary; allocating principal and income among charities; making a will in which any of these powers is exercised; applying income to the support of a dependent; effecting the enjoyment of the property after a ten-year period has elapsed; and ultimately paying income to the beneficiary. If a stranger trustee is named, the grantor may still have any of these powers.

Powers Relinquished by the Grantor

On the other hand, some powers are strictly taboo for grantors. If a grantor or any subordinate—such as a spouse, mother, father, sibling, child, employee, corporation in which the grantor has a significant amount of stock, or employee of such a corporation—has these powers, the grantor's tax bracket will be applied to the income from the trust fund. The following strictly taboo powers should be specifically prohibited in the trust itself. In preparing a trust for a minor, most attorneys do this automatically. The most significant of the taboos are:

1. The power to buy, exchange, or deal with the trust income or principal without an adverse party's consent for less than adequate consideration.
2. The power to borrow from the trust without adequate interest or security except when there is an independent trustee with the power to make loans to anyone without regard to interest security.
3. Borrowing money from the trust without completely repaying the loan, together with interest, before the beginning of the tax year.
4. The power to administer the trust in a nonfiduciary capacity without the consent of a fiduciary, such as the power to vote the stock of a corporation to control

investment of a trust fund and the power to substitute one type of trust property for another.

Exercising any of these powers can cause the income to be taxed at the grantor's tax bracket and rate.

The grantor's bracket and rate will also be applied if the grantor causes the income of the trust to be distributed to himself or his spouse, to be held or accumulated for distribution to himself or his spouse, or to be applied to the payment of insurance premiums on his or her life or that of the spouse.

If the parent grantor merely wishes to control when and whether the income or principal is paid to the child during the course of the trust for emergency needs, he or she can do so without any adverse tax consequences. That portion used for the child will be taxed to the parent. Parents might also wish to control the investments, but they cannot do so without breaking the "grantor" rules and affecting the tax benefits of the trust.

For example, if a father is named trustee and his child has a medical emergency, under the terms of the trust the father can decide to invade the principal. Only the amount actually used for the child's medical expenses will be taxed at the father's bracket and rate. But if no medical emergency arises and no use of principal is made, no tax is applied except at the trust rate for the child's bracket. On the other hand, if the trust allows the father to make investment decisions to the extent that he continually exchanges property, the entire trust would be tainted, and it is likely that the tax bracket and rate applied would be that of the father, not the child.

STRATEGY ROUNDUP

When you step back a moment from the morass of rules surrounding the child's trust, you can see why its popularity is growing:

1. It permits you to put money in trust for your child yet keep more control than with any other type of account.
2. Gifts under $10,000 are excluded from gift taxation.
3. The money and all its growth are out of your estate and not subject to estate tax.
4. The trust is simple to set up and cost-effective. The lawyers' fees are reasonable since the language is straightforward. (You'll find an example in Appendix B.)
5. Should you need the money, you can take it out. No one will stop you as they would with a UGMA or UTMA account. If you use the money for yourself, however, or to discharge a legal obligation to the child, the income will be taxed at your bracket.
6. If you maintain "too much" control over the funds, your tax bracket will apply. But:
7. This may not be so bad as many parents have brackets lower than the trust's and the same as their children's. This is frequently the case, not only for child stars but in families with businesses where grandparents have already given substantial interest to their grandchildren.

Despite these advantages, most of us waited a long time for an even simpler method of transferring funds to children while keeping control over investing and other matters. There's good news: Such a device is just now emerging into popularity—the family limited partnership.

·9·

The Family Limited Partnership

Once in a while a legal document comes along that seems like a miracle solution to many of the financial problems families face. Legal insiders consider the Family Limited Partnership (FLP) to be just such a document.

With an FLP, you name yourself, your spouse, or another family member as general partner (GP). The GP has the power to run a business, trade stock, sell real estate, or manage any other assets in the FLP.

The other, limited partners (LPs) have no such powers, but they are the ones who actually own most of the assets. For example, the GP may own 5 percent of the assets with the remainder equally divided among three children who are LPs.

An FLP can:

- be a powerful bargaining tool to settle with creditors
- be a device to transfer assets to loved ones and reduce

the taxes on the earnings from those assets
- help you implement the orderly transfer of assets to save estate taxes
- leave you in control of the assets you have transferred
- avoid the selection and cost of trustees

Here are some more benefits:

1. The creditors of the limited partners can get only a charging lien against the assets. They cannot seize or attach the assets until they have been paid out to the limited partners. The terms of the FLP should give the general partner the right to indefinitely reserve distribution. But here's the rub: Even though creditors can only impose a lien against the FLP's assets, it is the creditor that must pay the tax on any earnings from those assets. This doesn't avoid creditor claims, but it provides a great negotiating tool since the creditor is paying taxes on money it is not receiving.

2. If tax saving is your goal, an FLP could help you. The limited partners are taxed on the earnings of the assets. Every year the GP issues a K1 form to each LP, showing the income attributed to that partner. The LPs then pay the tax. This is an excellent way to shift taxes to a lower-bracket taxpayer and still manage the assets without a trust.

3. As for estate taxes, any assets now benefiting the LPs are outside the GP's estate. Yet the GP can keep control over management, distribution, and additions. There is no expensive outside trustee or hands-off irrevocable trust.

In short, the family limited partnership may very well take the place of the trust, where estate planning and creditor protection are goals. There is no need to use the Crummey provision to qualify gifts for the $10,000 exclusion.

The general partner (Mom, Dad, Grandpa) is usually the donor who sets up the assets. In the case of a trust, such a donor would have to appoint an independent trustee to handle the corpus of a trust in order to keep the assets out of the estate.

With an FLP, the estate exclusion remains in place even when control is in the hands of the donor as general partner. Changes in the provisions of the partnership document can be made without disturbing estate tax exclusions; that is, limited partners can be bought out or changed.

In fact, the creditor-protection features of an FLP are most likely to hold up under court scrutiny if the primary purpose of the partnership is estate planning.

All readers are invited to write or call my law firm for free information on family limited partnerships, limited liability partnerships, limited liability corporations, and offshore asset protection. Write: Friedland Fishbein Laifer & Robbins, 233 Broadway, New York, NY 10279, or call (212) 962-4888. For an example of a certificate filed when you complete a family limited partnership, see Appendix C.

·10·

Power of Attorney

A power of attorney is rarely thought of in connection with gift-giving. But next to the family limited partnership, it is probably the most powerful tool of all.

Here's the concept: The grantor chooses someone to be his attorney-in-fact and gives power in writing to that person. In effect, the grantor is appointing someone of his choosing to act on his behalf. The transfer can be executed without a lawyer.

The critical factor is that any third party, such as a bank, a brokerage house, or someone involved in a business transaction, must respect the authority of the attorney-in-fact over the assets as if it were the person himself.

So if Grandma wants to give a gift to grandson Sammy but she is in the hospital, she can appoint her daughter, Sammy's mom, to get the money from the bank and make the gift. The bank will hand over the funds upon presentation of the written power.

Horror stories of older folks signing a power of attorney, only to be fleeced of their meager fortune, crop up in the newspapers now and then. This fear, coupled with the notion that a power involves expensive lawyer's fees, keeps many people away from using powers. This is a mistake. In fact, every family should have a signed power between spouses and between adult children and their parents, in case of emergency.

Carefully selecting the type of power and, of course, relying on a trustworthy attorney-in-fact will prevent abuse. Most reports of abuse are unfortunate cases of distant relatives and strangers as attorneys-in-fact. Abuse of the elderly, a tragic crime like child or spousal abuse, is rare.

I hope that you will make the power of attorney part of your overall financial or estate plan. If the power of attorney is between loving family members, it is often not necessary to hire a lawyer to handle it.

Unlike the joint account, money subject to a power of attorney is still in the name of the original holder. Only the creditors and spouse of the grantor of the power can touch the money. Yet if the grantor should become ill, the money can be used for his welfare without court intervention.

If the grantor has created a trust but has failed to fund it, the attorney-in-fact can make the transfer. If an estate planner suggests that gifts be given to save estate taxes and the grantor is too ill to give them, the attorney-in-fact can do the work for him.

Today there are four different types of powers of attorney. The most popular is the *general durable power of attorney*. With this power, the attorney-in-fact can do anything on the grantor's behalf that the grantor could have done for himself. This includes filing income tax returns, making gifts, buying and selling securities, collecting rents, and much more.

Further, the power is "durable," which means that it lasts even if the grantor is incapacitated legally or physically to act on his own behalf. An Alzheimer's patient or a terminally ill patient can still have his money managed without court order through a power of attorney.

A second and today unpopular type is the *nondurable power of attorney*. Such powers are extinguished automatically if the grantor becomes incapacitated. They are most often used for a single transaction: for example, when a person goes on vacation and, while away, the spouse needs to close on a house. The nondurable power is rarely used because, as a general rule, it defeats the purpose that most of us have in transferring the power—to have someone care for our assets if we get sick.

The durability clause, however, is often missing from power-of-attorney forms that you might get at a bank or at a stationery store. You must write it in yourself. (See Appendix D for an example.) If you have already signed a power of attorney, check the language and look for the durability clause.

The third type is the *limited power of attorney*. It may be either durable or nondurable. A limited power allows the attorney-in-fact to do only one or a few different acts on behalf of the grantor. For example, it may allow the holder to create a trust and transfer assets to it. As a result, any potential donor can keep money in his own name and avoid gifting; yet he can empower another to make that gift at a particular time if he is unable to do so himself.

The fourth, and final, type of power is the *springing*

power of attorney. Such a power becomes valid only when the person is incapacitated. It is ineffective until the treating physician diagnoses a patient as "unable to comprehend." Springing powers are used by those who do not wish to relinquish control and are concerned that by signing a durable power, the attorney-in-fact may use it while the grantor still has the capacity to handle his own affairs. The springing power is often used by people without strong family ties who choose a professional or business-related person as their attorney-in-fact.

In Appendix D, you will find a power of attorney specifically designed by my law firm for those who want to grant limited gift-giving and funding power. Using this document in conjunction with a revocable trust, you can avoid probate and have your money handled if you are incapacitated (a power to such effect is written into the trust), while your gift-giving can be done without relinquishing one penny before you need to.

These two documents, the revocable trust and the gift-giving power, replace the dangerous joint account and do a lot more for you, safely. They permit grandparents to keep money for a grandchild's college tuition in their own name in the event that the child gets financial aid. (See page 85.) Yet should the child need the money at a time when the grandparent is incapacitated, funds can be distributed by the attorney-in-fact, who is usually the child's parent, the adult child of the grandparent.

·11·

A Short Course on the Cost of College

Here's chilling news: An Ivy League education, including room and board, costs over $25,000 a year in 1996. Nor are college costs expected to decline. *Money* magazine reported that in 1993–1994 the cost of private college tuition rose 7 percent, while public school tuition rose 10 to 12 percent. Today, the average cost of tuition at a non–Ivy League private college per year is $10,017; room and board is an additional $4,396; books are $508; lab fees are $911. Although higher education is not entirely out of reach, if you want your children to go to college, you need time or money or both.

Because of its cost, some people say that a college education is not worth the money. It has been hypothesized that, were a parent to give a child a sum of money equivalent to the cost of a college education, the child would earn more than with his earning capacity as a college graduate.

Actually, it's not so. Even conservative analysts conclude that a college degree can add approximately a quarter of a million dollars in earning power over a lifetime. Invest this amount at the same rate as the cost of the college degree, and the college grad is likely to be the lifetime winner. This is not to mention the self-esteem, lifestyle, variety of opportunities, and other nonmonetary considerations provided by a college education.

So don't let the nay-sayers, the jealous relatives, or the folks with something to sell dissuade you from helping your children to get a degree.

You may be surprised that I even address the issue of whether college is worth it. Perhaps in your family, as in mine, education is a life goal in itself, and the value of a college education is taken for granted. That may be so in your home but it surely is not everywhere, and we are all subject to outside influence. For example, at a recent conference of the nation's top investment newsletter writers, at least three referred in their speeches to the choice of forgoing college. They belittled the experience and pooh-poohed its importance. While all of them had degrees themselves, it's become fashionable to sneer at education—especially among the educated.

But the anti-academic movement runs deeper than the scorn of effete contrarians. The December 12, 1994, issue of *U.S. News & World Report* cited a leave of absence due to exhaustion taken by Neil Rudenstine, the president of Harvard University. The story told of the strenuous fund-raising and cost-cutting efforts of the academic-turned-administrator and implied that a new day is dawning when universities will be run by business people. Michigan State, for example, chose as its president M. Peter McPherson, formerly a top executive at Bank of America.

Academia is changing. Colleges once wielded major political and business influence, which meant a great deal to the future of their students. Getting an education was seen as just the beginning. Old school ties, alumni loyalty to students seeking jobs, and even pipelines to government were special benefits of higher education. But the ability of high-status Ivy League schools, which are also the most expensive, to deliver the contacts for which they are so famous may be changing. Today colleges may do better for your child if their present student body, rather than their past history, is top notch.

As parents, we must strike a balance between the new-fashioned idea that the American Dream need not include college and the old-fashioned idea that the most expensive and most historically prestigious schools are the best for your child's future.

Moreover, the public college is still a great educational bargain. You'll save a great deal of money by sending your child to a public university, with tuition averaging $2,137; room and board, $3,351; books $485; and lab fees $1,147.

No matter what approach you choose, you must start with a plan. That requires you to face facts, which is the first step toward financing your child's college education. The numbers can be frightening, but the clearer you are about what it's really going to cost, the more likely you are to make the grade.

HOW MUCH MONEY WILL YOU NEED?

To determine your future costs, calculate your children's educational needs. For each child, list the amount you will need for his first year of college. How do you figure the yearly cost? It depends on the college you expect him to attend. Choose a few colleges that seem likely choices, and call their bursars. The bursars will not only tell you the present tuition but will give you an idea of the projected costs. If your child is many years from attending college, you will need to project the future cost of tuition of both private and public colleges. (The College Planning Worksheet on page 78 will help you.) For further information on tuition, board, and room costs, you can write to:

Association of Independent Colleges and Universities
1717 Massachusetts Avenue, N.W.
Washington, DC 20036

American Association of Community and Junior
* Colleges*
One Dupont Circle, N.W., Suite 410
Washington, DC 20036

If a city or state school is what you have in mind, you can find out its costs by writing to:

National Association of State Universities and Land
* Grant Colleges*
One Dupont Circle, N.W., Suite 710
Washington, DC 20036

Calculating the Cost with a Sharp Pencil

For those who find ballpark numbers insufficient, here is a variation of a worksheet prepared by Scudder. (You can receive their booklet entitled "Investing for College—The Scudder Investor Series" by calling [800] 225-2470.)

College Planning Worksheet

Enter the following information	Example
1. Your child's age.	2
2. Number of years until college.	16
3. Current annual cost of the preferred college, if you know it. Otherwise, use either of these average figures:	
$ 6,720, for a public college	
$15,832, for a private college	$15,832
4. Inflation factor (based on number of years until college). Obtain the appropriate inflation factor from the Inflation Factor Tables located at the end of this Worksheet.*	3.20
5. Anticipated annual college cost (multiply line 3 by line 4).	$50,662
6. Total cost of college (multiply line 5 by the number of college years planned).	$202,650
7. Estimated amount of future income, loans, work-study income, and other sources expected to be used to meet college expenses.	$40,000
8. Net cost of college (subtract line 7 from line 6).	$162,650

---

* Inflation factors are based on the average annual increase of college tuition from 1982 through 1993, using data provided by the College Board. The average annual increase for public colleges over the last twelve years was 6.06 percent; for private colleges, the average increase for the same period was 7.53 percent.

Inflation Factor Tables

Public College

Years to College	1	2	3	4	5	6
Inflation Factor	1.06	1.12	1.19	1.27	1.34	1.42

Years to College	7	8	9	10	11	12
Inflation Factor	1.51	1.60	1.70	1.80	1.91	2.03

Years to College	13	14	15	16	17	18
Inflation Factor	2.15	2.28	2.42	2.56	2.72	2.88

Private College

Years to College	1	2	3	4	5	6
Inflation Factor	1.08	1.16	1.24	1.34	1.44	1.55

Years to College	7	8	9	10	11	12
Inflation Factor	1.66	1.79	1.92	2.07	2.22	2.39

Years to College	13	14	15	16	17	18
Inflation Factor	2.57	2.76	2.97	3.20	3.44	3.69

PLANNING TO MEET YOUR GOAL

The next step is to calculate how much you will need to invest each year, month, or quarter to meet your projected college costs. You'll base your calculations on your investments earning an 8 percent average annual return, with a 31 percent federal tax rate on income and other distributions. If your investment returns are lower than 8 percent a year on average, or if your investment distributions are taxed at a higher or lower rate, the amount of money you need to meet your goal will be affected.

Example

9. Enter the appropriate factor from the
   Periodic Investment Factor Table, at the
   end of this worksheet.   29.18

10. Annual investment amount (divide line 8
    on page 78 by line 9). $5,574

    or

    Monthly investment amount (divide line 10
    by 12). $ 465

    or

    Quarterly investment amount (multiply
    line 10 by 3). $1,394

Periodic Investment Factor Table

Years to College	1	2	3	4	5	6
Investment Factor	1.07	2.21	3.42	4.72	6.11	7.59

Years to College	7	8	9	10	11	12
Investment Factor	9.17	10.86	12.66	14.58	16.64	18.83

Years to College	13	14	15	16	17	18
Investment Factor	21.17	23.67	26.34	29.18	32.23	35.47

If the amounts on line 10 are "doable" for you, great! You can go right on to Chapters 12 and 13 and learn how to invest your monthly savings for college, or your one-time, lump-sum savings, to meet your goal.

But if the amounts in line 10 are well above your ability, there are several ways of defraying college costs. To describe each in detail is well beyond the scope of a book on giving and investing. The thorough Bibliography at the end, however, will help you further, as will the interview with a college aid adviser later in this chapter.

Still, I can't resist including a few of my own favorite college-financing strategies:

Two-Year College

You can send your child to a very fine two-year college, from which he will get an associate degree. These colleges cost about half as much per year as four-year colleges and universities. But all the credits your child earns from this college can be transferred if your child then applies to a four-year college to complete his junior and senior years. It is my experience that employers only look at the college from which you graduated, not at where you got all four years of your education.

Residency

A student who has reached the age of majority (eighteen in some states) may live and work in a state to establish residence. After a prescribed period of time (in some cases a year or less), the student is eligible to attend the state university, both as a self-supporting student and as a state resident, thereby qualifying for lower tuition.

ROTC

An Army Reserve Officers' Training Corps scholarship can provide as much as $33,000 over four years. To qualify, the student must be at least seventeen years old, a high school graduate, and a citizen of the United States. Although

ROTC is usually a four-year program, two-year programs are available for junior and community college students. Scholarships are also available to enlist for four years of active and two years of reserve duty after graduation. They pay full tuition, books, and college fees and a small monthly stipend for pocket money.

Awards of ROTC scholarships are based on merit. The student must do well on scholastic aptitude tests, show leadership ability in extracurricular and school activities, and do well in personal interviews. Application forms may be requested from April 1 of the student's junior year through November 15 and from January 15 to April 15. Write Army ROTC Scholarships, P.O. Box 12703, Philadelphia, PA 19134. If you are already enlisted, write Army ROTC Scholarships, Fort Monroe, VA 23651.

Other branches of the military also have extensive scholarship programs for both two- and four-year periods. The programs differ in the age at which the student must complete his college term.

For those already in the armed services, many tuition-assistance programs are available. In fact, most military advertisements seeking to recruit young people make their appeal on the basis of educational opportunities offered.

The child or spouse of a veteran who either died or was totally disabled because of military service may be entitled to an education benefit. For more information, write to the nearest office of the Veterans Administration (listed under U.S. Government in your phone book).

Loans and grants are also available to military dependents. For a list, send one dollar to the American Legion (National Emblem Sales, P.O. Box 1055, Indianapolis, IN 46206) and ask for the booklet "Need a Lift?"

Student Loans

A growing proportion of the college bill is now being shouldered by students themselves, in the form of low-interest student loans. For the most part, no interest accrues on these loans until graduation.

A student should be extremely cautious in taking out a loan, however. The amount may not seem like much initially, but it quickly adds up. A student who borrows $2,500 a year for four years will graduate with a $10,000 debt. I often prepare financial plans for doctors and lawyers who, after ten or more years of practice, are still paying off their student loans.

These loans may also be an excellent investment, however. They can enable the student to attend a more prestigious college, which could lead to better employment opportunities. Also, as their interest rates are low, parents might be able to help with making payments. (Although the loan is issued to the student, it actually helps the parents who are paying for college.)

Federal guaranteed student loans are available through many banks. The amount and your child's eligibility depend on your family's need and circumstances (including other children). The Federal Register lists levels of income that determine the expected family contribution. Families with incomes of $30,000 and less are generally eligible, while those with incomes of $75,000 and more are ineligible, but there is a wide gray area.

An IRA or Keogh

If your child will not be attending college until you are in retirement, you might want to save for college with an Individual Retirement Account (IRA) or Keogh account.

Your money will enjoy the power of tax-deferred compounding until withdrawal, when taxes are due only on the portion you withdraw. If you withdraw money from your IRA or Keogh before age 59½, however, the IRS assesses a 10 percent early-withdrawal penalty. So check to see whether you qualify for an *escape-hatch provision,* which permits you to withdraw a portion of your IRA without paying the early-withdrawal penalty.

The amount that can be withdrawn under the escape-hatch provision is based on your life expectancy and the assumed rate of return. For example, a fifty-five-year-old with $100,000 in an IRA could withdraw approximately $8,800 a year, assuming an annual return of 8 percent. If you set up such a payment schedule, you have to stick with it for five years or until you turn 59½, whichever is longer. Ask your accountant or tax adviser to help figure out whether the escape-hatch rules works for you.

The problem of paying for college tuition has finally reached Washington. We may soon see federal legislation that will allow penalty-free withdrawals for college tuition from pension programs or IRAs. It helps to write your congressperson to give your support to such measures.

A 401(k) Plan

If you have a 401(k) Plan, you can favorably borrow from that pension plan and pay for the children's education with it. So when you contribute to the 401(k), you are really planning for them, saving taxes, and ensuring your own future all at the same time. By investing money in your own future through pensions, you are also enhancing your child's ability to pay for college aid.

When you plan your college-tuition goals, don't be alarmed. Don't add up all the figures that I gave you, decide it's too much money, and not bother to do college planning at all. On the contrary, the earlier you start and the more prudent you are, the more likely you are to be able to send your child to a wonderful school.

INTERVIEW WITH KALMAN A. CHANY, THE GURU OF FINANCIAL AID FOR COLLEGE AND POSTGRADUATE STUDIES

Kalman A. Chany is a fee-based, independent, financial aid consultant who has clients all over the United States and in Europe. He has helped scores of parents maximize their ability to get financial aid. Unlike many consultants, he does not sell insurance or any other financial product. His office and telephone number may be found on the Resources page. A financial aid consultation will generally cost from $250 to $1,000. My main interest in this interview is the nexus between gift-giving and eligibility for college aid.

> Q: When is the best time to seek counseling to deter-mine whether it's possible to get aid to help pay for college?
> A: By tenth grade or the beginning of eleventh grade. Planning is the key, so parents must get advice well before the base year.
> Q: Explain base year.
> A: The aid formula looks at the year preceding the year for which you seek aid. Your ability to pay for this year is based on last year's earnings.

Q: Is it really possible for middle-class people to get aid?

A: Absolutely. Many fail to get aid because they misunderstand the forms and the process. Early planning can make a big difference in the way you structure your assets and income during the four years that really count.

Q: In your book, *The Princeton Review Student Access Guide to Paying for College* (Villard Books 1995), you make it clear that titling accounts in a child's name could be throwing away money. How so?

A: More or less, thirty-five cents on the dollar in a child's name will be expected to be spent on college. Fifty cents of every dollar of his income. Parent's assets are counted at a bit over five cents on the dollar, and grandparents' assets are not expected to be spent at all.

Q: Should parents keep money in their own name despite a possible tax savings if held in the child's name?

A: In many cases, yes. If there is any hope of aid, keep the money in the parents' accounts.

Q: What about trusts?

A: Unless the trustee need not transfer any assets to the student, which must be determined on a case-by-case basis, trusts for kids are counted in the same way as the UGMA/UTMA—the money is the child's.

Q: What about family limited partnerships?

A: They are very new. Income to a child shown on a K1 will likely be counted. Otherwise, to rely on them would be an aggressive strategy. They require very individual planning.

Q: What assets of parents are not counted in determining need for aid?

A: Under the so-called federal formula, equity in a home; insurance products such as annuities and cash value of life insurance policies; and money in all types of pensions and IRAs. But never base your financial investments solely on a strategy to get aid. Make sure they are sound in themselves.

Q: What if money has already been gifted to a child? Is it too late to get the money back into the parents' or grandparents' name?

A: In many cases it is. Once again we would have to look at whether the family has a need for the child that is not a legal obligation, such as study abroad. If money is transferred back, it must be done correctly, not just to qualify for aid.

Q: What if the funds are used to pay for a private high school.

A: This is a gray area. In some cases it might be justified.

·12·

Investing for Children

Experience shows that money is usually invested for children in two particular circumstances. First, the children may inherit or for some other reason (such as divorce settlement) receive a lump-sum amount. Usually, this sum is received at an unplanned, unpredictable time. Second, a parent or grandparent decides to invest small amounts over a long period of time to pay for college tuition. In this chapter, we will deal with investing small amounts over long periods of time. In the next, we will look at lump-sum and college-only investment strategies.

You don't have to be Warren Buffett to know that the longer you save at the best yield, the more money you will have. The following chart shows how much you will accumulate by a one-time investment of $1,000 at 8 percent interest compounded daily:

1 year	$1,084.49
2 years	$1,275.49

5 years	$1,500.14
10 years	$2,250.41
20 years	$5,064.33

To calculate how long it will take an investment to double (before taxes), simply divide the interest rate into the number 72. At 8 percent interest, $1,000 will become $2,000 in nine-years (72 divided by 8). This so-called "rule of 72" is a quick way to figure when you are speaking to brokers about investments that have fixed yields or interest rates. It's not much of a help if stocks are your investment choice.

STAY WITH A DISCIPLINED INVESTMENT PLAN

The key to making regular small investing work and to reaping the beneficial effects of *reinvested dividends* is to start now. For example, making a $1,200 investment ($100 a month) each year, at a hypothetical constant average annual rate of 10 percent, can accumulate to $60,191 after eighteen years. (To simplify this example, we've assumed that the money is invested continuously and that no taxes are taken from the investment earnings. Taxes might have to be paid each year, depending on whether the account is registered, say, in the parent's name rather than the child's.)

In choosing investments for a college education, remember that your investment dollar has certain characteristics.

- Your investment dollar is long-term. That is, your investments can grow over a long period of time and need not be liquid.
- Because of devices available that lower the income tax charged on investment income, your investment dol-

lar may go to assets that yield taxable income or capital gains, instead of ones that are tax-free.
- Because you are not expected to use principal or income until the college years, your investment dollar can go to assets chosen for their growth potential.

Thus, you can look for an investment that is illiquid, taxable, long-term and growth-oriented.

You need a goal. Are you trying to target paying for 100 percent of the college tuition and room and board for your children? If you know that now, you can find the answer to the question, "How do you invest the money that you are planning to give the children?"

If you can set aside as much as $50,000 or $75,000, your best investments will be different from those who are planning merely to give them a little bit of a head start and pay for the first year of education.

There are two schools of thought when it comes to investing for college. One school makes predictability and safety the priority. Investments like the zero-coupon bond and College Sure can provide safety. This school of thought is discussed in Chapter 13.

The other holds that if you start early enough, the stock market is the place to be because of its historically excellent returns over long periods of time. It is this philosophy that we will examine here.

STOCK MARKET INVESTING

Ibbotson, a Chicago-based research firm, conducted studies on how *quickly* money made money in various investments over a period from 1926 to the present. This, in a nutshell, is what they discovered: The best growth pattern (or fastest pace) of any investment has been small capitalized companies, called "small cap stocks." Over time, nothing has done better than money put in mutual funds or individual companies that are small and growing. Next in terms of pace were investments in large companies. Next came long-term government bonds, and finally treasury bills. The value of a one 1926 dollar investment in small cap stocks would be $1,277.45 in 1990. In large-company Standard & Poor's 500 stocks, it would be about half that, or $517.50. In long-term government bonds, the value of the dollar would only be $17.99. And in treasury bills, you would have gotten back $10.43 for every dollar that you invested from 1926 to the present. So the range is from $10.43 to $1,277.45!

This study is factually accurate, and in the financial-planning community there is little disagreement over its conclusions. If you are going to invest for a young child, you want to buy small cap stocks of individual companies or through mutual funds. For your newborn to age six, who has twelve to eighteen years before college, you will want to invest in a stock market index mutual fund whose objective is small cap growth, such as the Vanguard 500 Index Trust, which follows the 500 companies of the Standard & Poor's 500.

The array of mutual funds is quite broad. You can become a unit owner in small cap stock funds, either domestic or international; in aggressive growth stock funds; or in S&P 500 index funds with as little as a hundred-dollar investment. If you would prefer not to pay a commission you can consider no-load (no-commission) funds. How do you find out about these funds? There are so many mutual funds—as of last count, we totalled 5,500 different ones. You can get recommendations and examples from your financial planner, or from books like McGraw-Hill's *Business Week's Guide to Mutual Funds,* which is updated every year.

Your Investment Objective	Type of Fund	These Funds Invest Primarily In
Maximum capital growth	Small cap growth	Common stocks with the potential for very rapid growth. May employ certain aggressive strategies
Capital growth with modest risk	Large cap growth	Common stocks with long-term growth potential
Current income and capital Growth	Growth and income; equity income	Common stocks with potential for high dividends and capital appreciation
High current income	Fixed income	High-yield bonds
Tax-free income	Municipal bonds	A broad range of municipal bonds
Current income and protection of principal	General or government money market accounts or bond funds	Money market instruments, treasuries and government bonds

As you begin to investigate mutual funds, you may find yourself overwhelmed by the many choices. Here is a brief synopsis of types of funds.

Potential for Capital Growth	Potential for Current Income	Stability of Principal
Very high	Very low	Low to very low
High to very high	Very low	Low
Moderate	Moderate	Low to moderate
Very low	High to very high	Low to moderate
Low to moderate	Moderate to high	Moderate
None	Moderate to high	Very high

Adapted from a chart by the Mutual Fund Education Alliance

Note that these funds are not guaranteed to increase in value and even have periods of high volatility. If you do not want to experience ups and downs in your college portfolio, read on to Chapter 13.

Once you have selected a type of fund, which of the many "brands" should you choose?

I subscribe to what I call the "Blue Suit Theory of Investing." With a blue suit, you can't go wrong in many situations. So, too, with the types of funds I recommend.

INVESTING ACCORDING TO THE AGE OF YOUR CHILD

Clearly, with stocks doing best over time and interest-certain investments giving the most safety when time is short, your strategy will change depending on the age of your child. This is the case for parents and grandparents investing for any future goal of a child, including college.

For those with twelve to eighteen years until money is needed for college, past performances have shown us that it's very appropriate to take a risk.

For those with seven to thirteen years before college, you want slightly less risk. Why? you may well ask. Why not go for the gold no matter how many years we have left before our child goes to college? Why not go with what has proved to make the most money?

The answer is that successful performance in the stock market depends on continuous investment over a long period of time. Stocks often lose money over short periods of time. When you have only five to eleven years left to invest, you might run into a two-, three-, or even five-year bad patch in the market. If you do, you will not reach your goal. So you must reduce the risk. That means moving into blue-chip stocks, more balanced funds, and funds that offer growth and perhaps pay dividends as well. Let's say that you have been investing in more aggressive funds ever since your six-year-old daughter was born. Should you switch to lower-risk investments when she nears her seventh birthday? The answer is probably no. The very fact that you have a long-term investment time-line permits you to leave your money in the more aggressive funds.

But people who are just starting to invest when their child is already seven years old should not take the most aggressive approach but rather a more moderate and balanced approach.

Finally, if you are beginning to invest just four years or so before your child goes to college, you must sacrifice the possibility of stock market gains for the certainty of "targeted" investments. These are investments that give you a guarantee that they will be worth a certain amount after a specified period of time. With targeted investments you can know how much money will your money make by the exact time your children enroll in college. Targeted investments include corporate bonds, municipal bonds (if your tax bracket is high), College Sure, treasury bills, and zero-coupon bonds, because they all have maturity dates. With these investments, you can target the amount you will actually have ready for your children. (See Chapter 13 for more on these investments.)

Once again, if you have started early, do not switch your investments at this time, unless you have already reached your goal and you want only to preserve your capital. The conservative approach is mainly for those who started late and are trying to make the best run they possibly can four years or so before college.

If you have only two years or one year left before college you are better off making no investment at all. The reason is that the likelihood of your money growing to any great extent (even by 19 percent, the record high for certain very aggressive mutual funds) is offset by the fact that by putting money in your child's name just as he is going to seek financial aid, you probably will be costing him eligibility for that aid, as well as grants, loans, and certain scholarships. Much as you would like to show your love or make a gesture to help him with college, keep the money in your own name. There is one exception: When the amount is a big gift, particularly by grandparents divesting themselves of assets to save estate taxes.

INVESTMENT ROUNDUP

Preschool (age 0 to 4). With fourteen to seventeen years before your child starts college, you should accept a higher level of risk to aim for maximum growth. Therefore, your portfolio could include 30 percent in an aggressive growth fund, 30 percent in an international fund, and 40 percent in a growth-and-income fund.

Elementary school (age 5 to 9). With nine to thirteen years before your child starts college, you can still emphasize growth, but you may want to moderate your risk somewhat by shifting some assets into income funds. Therefore, your conservative growth portfolio could put 30 percent in an international fund, 30 percent in a growth fund invested in quality companies, 30 percent in a growth-and-income fund, and 10 percent in an intermediate-term corporate bond fund.

Junior high school (age 10 to 13). With five to eight years before your child starts college, your portfolio should still emphasize growth. Now, however, you can shift to an increasing emphasis on income and capital preservation, giving you a low-to-moderate risk profile, with 20 percent in an international fund, 30 percent in a quality growth fund, 40 percent in a growth-and-income fund, and 10 percent in an intermediate-term corporate bond fund.

High school (age 14 to 18). With no more than four years until your child starts college, the emphasis on income and capital preservation increases in order to lock in gains made earlier. However, you'll still want some growth to help keep the portfolio ahead of inflation, both now and during the four years your child is in college. Therefore, 10 percent might be put into an international fund, 20 percent in a growth-and-income fund, 20 percent in a balanced fund investing in stocks and bonds, 30 percent in an intermediate-term corporate bond fund, and 20 percent in short-term bonds or certificates of deposit.

THE PRUDENT PERSON RULE

If you are a fiduciary, please remember the Prudent Person Rule. Do not take risks with the money of minors. As a fiduciary, you are personally liable for losses as well as taxes. To be sure, you are liable for losses only if you could have foreseen them and you were not negligent in making the investment. Thus, you are not responsible if you made a perfectly natural or appropriate investment-grade decision and took a loss. But if you did take risks, such as putting money in commodity trading or highly speculative mutual funds, you could have a personal liability. Further, you have no real reason to take such risks. Let the children grow up, then hand them their nest egg. The rest will be up to them.

Some planners, many parents, and most grandparents believe that investing for college is sui generis, a species of investing all its own that requires above all safety and steadiness.

For those who would like to avoid all risk, even at the expense of total return, some special college-friendly investments will allow you to do just that. The next chapter presents a menu of such ideal college-investing vehicles.

·13·

College-Specific Investments and Lump-Sum Planning

Because of the special characteristics of college planning—a targeted goal for a targeted date, a low-tax-bracket investor (the child), and often a long time-line—a variety of investments have been identified by financial planners as most suitable for college investing. Many of these investments are time-honored vehicles that happen to fit into a college savings program. Others are investments created and marketed especially for college savings.

In Chapter 12 we looked at some proven methods of successful investing for college over time. But they were not without risk. Even if you began early, eventually you will want to move your dollars to more guaranteed, targeted investments. Or perhaps you have a lump sum to invest while your child is very young and want certainty from the start. To consider your options, you'll need to be familiar with these college-oriented investment products.

ZERO-COUPON BONDS

To understand the zero-coupon bond, you must understand a bit about bonds in general.* Happily, the zero-coupon is not difficult to understand. A bond represents a debt owed to you by the U.S. government, a corporation, a municipality, or whatever entity issued the bond. All bonds have a face value, called par. Par is the amount you will get if you hold the bond until its maturity date and then redeem it. Each bond has a date at which this redemption can take place, known as the maturity date. In addition to par, every bond has a *coupon*. A coupon is the amount of interest you get while you hold the bond.

When you bought your bond you received a promise to be repaid (at par) for the loan, with interest (the coupon amount). You thereby became a creditor. For you, the creditworthiness of the borrower is very important. That's why bonds are rated for safety by several companies. Your broker will tell you whether your bond has an A rating or less.

If interest rates in general fall below the rate on your bond coupon, you can sell the bond at a profit above what you paid. If interest rates rise above your coupon rate, the value of the bond will fall below what you paid for it.

---

* For readers with a keen interest in investing their own income, an excellent source of information is *The Bond Book* by Annette Thau (Probus Press, 1992). It explains the intricacies of all types of bond investing in simple terms.

However, you will always get back the par value if you wait until the maturity date to redeem your bond.

The zero-coupon bond has all the characteristics of other bonds, except that the interest-bearing coupon has been stripped from it. The bond pays no interest for that reason it is sold to you at a discount (at an amount below par). In general, the longer you are prepared to tie up your money, the more discount you get and the more growth you receive for your dollar. At the maturity date of the bond, you will receive its full face value. The difference between what you paid for and what you will get is your profit.

The growth of the par value is reflected every year as a gain (accreted value). And that gain is taxed as ordinary income each year, although you receive no actual income. To lessen the amount of this tax, the bonds, when you purchase them, can be transferred to your child and taxed at the child's lower tax rate.

For example, if a two-paycheck family with a two-year-old child were to purchase a zero-coupon bond for $10,000 and place the bond in a trust for their child, they would pay no gift tax since the gift is worth exactly $10,000. (See Chapter 2.)

The parents pay no capital gains tax, and the growth is declared as income to the entity (parent, UGMA, trust, etc.) that holds the bond. If the trust has no other assets that generate income, it will pay very little income tax at all. In families where tax savings are of great importance because both the parents and the children are in a top tax bracket, zero-coupon municipal bonds can be bought tax-free. (See Chapter 2 on the kiddie tax.)

Aside from its tax aspects, a zero-coupon bond is considered appropriate for college planning because it yields a predictable amount at a predictable time. If you invest $4,500 at current rates for seventeen years, you will receive $30,000. If you invest $4,000 at current rates for thirty years, you will receive $100,000.

These investments are not risk-free, however. If the bond is of low quality, the borrower may default and the principal may be lost. A rise in interest rates may depress the value of the bond. If you have to sell the bond before its maturity date, you may see a loss if the market's interest is high. The moral is: Use only money that you believe you will not need for emergencies or other purposes to invest in zero-coupon bonds.

One cautionary note: The zero-coupon bonds you buy may be *callable*, which means the issuer has the right to redeem them before their maturity, usually to take advantage of declining interest rates. Not all zeros are callable: For example, treasury zeros are not. But if the municipality, corporation, or other entity that issued yours calls them in early, you may have to reinvest the money at what could be a substantially lower rate of return.

If you're considering a municipal or corporate zero-coupon bond, ask your broker or bond dealer to make sure it is noncallable. Or if it is callable, make sure that you know the earliest possible "call date," so that you can plan for the eventuality.

You don't want to make a good investment that two, three, or four years before your child is about to go to college, is called early and cashed in. Therefore, when studying zero-coupon bonds, look for maturity dates that accord with the year of your child's entry into college, and look for noncallability.

BACCALAUREATE BONDS

An investment akin to the zero-coupon bond but specifically designed for college planning, is the baccalaureate bond. It is actually an ordinary zero-coupon municipal bond. Only fifteen or twenty states issue them at any given time. To use them you must not only be a resident of the state but have your child attend the state university. They work like any other tax-free zero except that your state will give you a discount on the tuition if you enroll in the state university and pay with these bonds.

The evident purpose of such bonds is to enhance the borrowing power of the state. Take care to buy only if your child will definitely go to the state school and if the bond rating is investment grade.

SAVINGS BONDS

U. S. government savings bonds give you a tax benefit if you use them to pay for college, but usually they do not have a high enough return to be worth your while. But if your taxable income is less than $60,000 for an individual or less than $96,000 for a couple at the time you redeem your EE savings bonds, the interest you earned from them is partially or fully exempt from federal taxation, if you use the money to pay for college. So if your combined income as a couple is $96,000 or less, or if you're a single parent with $60,000 or less in yearly income, you can get a great tax break by using EEs for college. This investment should be considered only under those circumstances. Once again, you will generally do better if you invest in a small cap or Standard & Poor's 500 mutual fund starting very early in your child's life. Information is available free of charge by writing to:

Bureau of the Public Debt
Division of Customer Services
300 13th Street, S.W.
Washington, DC 20239-0001

COLLEGE SURE

The College Sure is a special product that has been created just for people who want to get their kids to college. All comprehensive books written on the topic of gifting to children mention this program. It is a certificate of deposit, issued by a bank located in Princeton, New Jersey, that was chartered especially to issue specific certificates of deposit. At present it serves people from all over the country and internationally as well.

What makes College Sures different from the CDs issued by any other bank? They are geared to the cost of college—the average tuition cost at the time your child will attend.

You select whether you would like to save for one year, two years, or four years of college. The College Sure bank works out a formula that tells you the amount you must save on a monthly or lump-sum basis in order to reach your goal. And they guarantee that if the cost of tuition goes up more than their estimate, they will pay for the college "unit" (the period of time you wished to cover, i.e., semester, year, four years).

The formula they use is based on inflationary factors, in keeping with your child's age and the type of school in which you are interested. They then give you a college-savings program. For the most part, the returns are not high.

The attraction of College Sures is the guarantee that if college tuition and inflation run away, the tuition will be paid as long as you keep your periodic-saving promise.

Recently, many corporations have instituted College Sure programs as an employee benefit.

PREPAID TUITION PROGRAMS

Some states offer prepaid tuition programs. They are going out of favor, and at the moment most of them are in the West: New Mexico and Wyoming. But Alabama, Ohio, and several other states are considering such plans at this writing. In these programs you select the school and prepay the tuition at a frozen cost. When your child finally does go to school, the tuition will be covered. If your child does not go to school, is not accepted in that school, or flunks out, you get a refund. But there is an administrative charge, so you don't get all your money back.

Because this money is invested for you, the IRS has gotten into the act and seems to be killing the project. They have done two important things of which you should be aware. One, they require that you pay income tax on the growth of the prepaid tuition as it is invested for you over the years. And two, under certain circumstances, if your child does go to the college and does take advantage of the savings, the IRS can tax the child. On what, you might ask? On the difference between what he would have paid and the low amount he actually did pay—in other words, on a phantom income. These programs are not generally in favor, as I said, but they do work if your child is serious about attending a state school.

Alert: Court cases followed by new legislation may reverse the negative tax rules that have nearly ruined these programs. Stay in touch with the admissions office of your state school to follow the fate of the program.

RENTAL REAL ESTATE

A very fashionable strategy that has been written about in many best-selling books is the strategy of buying a frat house, an apartment, or a two-family home in the town where your child will be attending college. The idea is that your child will live there at no charge. Of course, room and board are now paid for. The child will manage the building, pick and choose friends, and rent out the property to them. The income from that property, lo and behold, will help defray your tuition charges. You might even take out a loan against that property, a mortgage, and use the lump sum to pay the tuition for the four-year period.

Does this strategy work? It can, under certain circumstances. The property you buy must be Tiffany-stamped in quality, and it must be in an area where the need for off-campus housing is rampant so you have no vacancies. It would be very useful if you accumulate equity in the property, which means no borrowing before the time of tuition payment. And, of course, it would help a lot if your child really could live there, rent the place, manage the building, and keep everybody, including you and the tax collector, happy. Good luck!

LIFE INSURANCE

Life insurance salesmen have long recommended buying insurance and then either borrowing against it or surrendering the policy to withdraw the cash value for college. Further, they often suggest that parents make a large lump-sum premium payment to "bury" cash, equity in the home, and the like into a policy. The "strategy" is to make you appear needier and less able to pay on financial aid forms. (See Chapter 11.) These strategies neither work nor make good financial sense. The investment potential of these policies is not as great as other assets that do not also guarantee you a death benefit. But life insurance to assure continuity and security when a parent dies is a critical part of gifting to children. Read on to become an insider in the world of insurance.

·14·

Insurance to Build an Inheritance

Insurance is a vast topic. Luckily we deal here only with insurance purchased as a gift for a child to create an inheritance or an estate. Insurance purchased to replace the income of the main breadwinner is a different and more important consideration. For information on this topic see my book *Making Up for Lost Time* (Hearst, 1994) and *Making the Most of Your Money*, by Jane Bryant Quinn (Simon & Schuster, 1991).

If you wish to create a large estate for your children by placing their gifts into an insurance policy, here are some choices, each one with different features.

UNIVERSAL LIFE INSURANCE

In this kind of policy, you don't have to pay a fixed premium. It allows you to adjust your premium and the frequency of that premium. The premium goes to fund two separate things: a death benefit, and a separate account that grows at an interest rate, just as it might be if you'd invested in CDs or treasuries. The idea is that by the time the child is college age, you will have built up a cash value in that policy against which you can borrow. Since it's borrowing, it is tax-free for you. You pay the tuition. But you never pay back the money you borrowed. Instead, the death benefit that the child or other beneficiary would eventually receive upon your death is reduced. Meanwhile, the credited interest has grown over the years without your paying any income tax on it. In fact, you never will. If you don't cash in the policy but allow it to merge into a death benefit and if you plan your estate properly, you will end up with a tax-free estate in the amount of the death benefit minus the amount you borrowed.

FLEXIBLE VARIABLE LIFE INSURANCE

This is almost the same thing as universal life insurance, with one significant difference: Your account value depends not on your credited interest rate but on the performance of certain stocks. In other words, it varies. There are very few guarantees. In fact, the account could be much lower than you expect. You're taking a chance. As you already know, however, while stocks are a greater risk, they have always outperformed interest rates—as found by the Ibbotson study, which covered the years 1926 to the present. Once again, as the cash value in your policy grows, it grows tax-free, with no capital gains or income tax. If it has accumulated enough, you can borrow against it to pay for college. That borrowing is also tax-free.

Let me give you the downside. A great deal of your

premium—which is, of course, the amount of money that is working for you—goes to the death benefit. The death benefit does not pay college tuition unless you die. For tuition-payment purposes, you are generally much better off with a simple term insurance policy that will pay your child's tuition in the event of your early demise.

Second, the fees are very heavy, and they are hidden in the premium. Many of you have struggled with load and no-load mutual funds and often have selected a no-load fund because you did not want your investment dollar to go to commissions. I make no judgment about this. I personally look at the overall performance rather than cost, even though it can be significant. In universal life and flexible variable life insurance, however, you do not realize the size of your load. Every year, starting when you first take out this policy, a significant percentage of your premium goes to management fees, sales fees, and other charges. As a result, even with good performance and good credited interest, you may very well make far less in the cash benefit than you would if you invested the money in another way.

Those of you who like a one-step package—death benefit for the children, cash value for their college education, and tax savings—should look into universal life and flexible variable life. And those of you who plan to buy a straight or whole life policy, which can be expensive, may prefer the investment style policies of universal life and flexible variable life.

SURVIVORSHIP WHOLE LIFE INSURANCE

These policies, sometimes called "second to die" or "joint and survivor," are a premier tool for estate creation. Under these policies, both parents must be dead before the benefit is paid. The insurance is not available to widows or widowers. The insureds must be a married couple (parents or grand-parents). If there is a medical problem with one member of the couple, it is much easier to get underwriting than if each applied separately. Perhaps the person would ordinarily be uninsurable, yet together they may very possibly get this kind of policy. Because there are two ages to work with, the early death of one spouse poses much less of a risk for the insurance company, since they don't have to pay until both parties are gone. That also means that the cost of the insurance is far lower than any whole life policy. Yet it builds up cash-surrender value very well.

The plan can be even less costly if term insurance is included in the formula. Your insurance professional could structure a plan for you with 50 percent term insurance and 50 percent whole life. Unlike term insurance, if you die by age seventy or later, the policy is not canceled. And it is economical. A $5,000-a-year premium, for example, for a forty-five-year-old couple can build a million-dollar legacy for their children. It is something worth looking into. Very rarely do couples in their thirties have the extra money to build such a dynasty. But if you do, you might be able to stop paying the premium in seven to ten years, having built up several million dollars that can never be taken from your children. That's quite a legacy!

It's worth looking into illustrations for universal, whole life, and term life second-to-die policies. They differ widely in price and in the security you get that the premium will begin to pay for the policy after a period of time. Term life is the cheapest but becomes very expensive if kept up for many years. Universal is more expensive but accumulates better cash surrender value and may be less expensive in the long run if you plan to hold it to build a death benefit rather than just covering the risk of an early death. Whole life is the most expensive, but accumulates the greatest cash surrender value.

Grandparents in their sixties and in good health can also leave a very handsome inheritance with the use of second-to-die policies. After the age of seventy, the policies become expensive, and they may not be in keeping with or appropriate to your plan. Nevertheless, it never hurts to see an illustration of how this extraordinary policy works if your purpose is to give an inheritance to your children or grandchildren. And, of course, the death benefit can be held in trust for minors, with a trustee handing out and distributing the benefits throughout their lifetime or as you dictate in the trust.

CHARITABLE TRUST WITH REPLACEMENT POLICY

A charitable trust coupled with an insurance policy can be a mighty estate-creation and tax-saving tool.

If you would like to create a major inheritance for your child but are unable to use an irrevocable trust because you don't want to give up the use and income from the money you have, consider a charitable trust. Here's how they work. You transfer your assets to that trust, naming your favorite charity as a beneficiary. The assets are liquidated directly after the title transfers to the charity. You become the beneficiary of the income, and the charity becomes the beneficiary of the principal, but only when you die. Because it is a charitable bequest, there are no taxes whatsoever: no estate taxes, and no capital gains taxes when the charity sells or liquidates your assets and turns them into cash. The only tax you pay is when you receive income on a monthly or annuity basis from the trustee of the trust.

Where are your children in this picture? You take the extra income that the charity is giving you on a monthly or periodic basis and pay premiums for a whopping insurance policy, which is also held in a tax-free trust for your children or grandchildren. Charitable giving works best when the grandparents are on the young side, healthy, and highly insurable. It is a gift-giving program worth considering.

RENEWABLE TERM

Renewable Term is the simplest form of insurance and the cheapest, at least initially. It gives your family only a death benefit. You select the amount you want your family to inherit at the time of your death. You pay a premium, which normally increases annually and is determined by your age and in some cases your health and sex. The policy will automatically terminate at the end of the stated period. If you haven't died, you have gambled and lost. You paid the premiums without receiving any benefits. The policy itself has no value other than that death benefit. This is the same concept as automobile or fire insurance. If you have no fire, you get nothing out of your insurance except peace of mind.

Remember that the death benefit is taxable to your estate. Many people are not aware of this, although we should all be taught this fact from the cradle. But avoiding the tax is really quite simple. Here's how. If you designate your beneficiary as the owner of the policy, then upon your death the face value of the policy will go to your beneficiary directly rather than fall into your estate and be taxed. The only catch is the usual one: You can't change your mind. Because you have made the beneficiary the owner, you are stuck with that beneficiary for life. If the beneficiary is your child and you are estranged, the only thing you can do is stop making payments and let the policy lapse, if you don't want to protect the child. But this catch should not deter you. In the normal case, you can save a great deal of estate tax.

Here again, you do not own the policy at date of death. The *benefit* is paid tax-free to a trust or corporation and is distributed according to the terms of the trust instrument or shareholder agreement.

Other features of the term policy are that its cost *increases* as you get older, and its renewability—the right to get a new one when the term expires—decreases with increasing age. Why? The insurance company wants to make the odds a little better for itself. If you are older, you are more likely to die sooner. Therefore, the premium is greater. After a while, for example, at age sixty-five or seventy, the insurance company doesn't want to play anymore.

But don't be alarmed. According to the National Insurance Consumers Organization (NICO), only 3 percent of term insurance is ever paid out. Ninety-seven percent of policies lapse before a death claim is made.

STRAIGHT OR WHOLE LIFE INSURANCE

This type of insurance is a much more expensive method of obtaining life insurance. Other and better methods of saving money are to use a bank and not an insurance company, or to try a variable life plan. Some good things, however, can be said about straight life insurance. One is that the policy cannot be canceled: You will be able to renew it all your life. The premiums start high and stay high—but they never increase. The policy accumulates a cash-surrender value. This means that if you cancel the policy, some money will come back to you. It isn't much compared with what you have paid, despite what insurance people may try to tell you. They'll likely show you how much you'll pay every year as a premium, compare it with the surrender value, then compare that with term insurance to show that you got a real bargain. Look at this:

Age 35
Whole life premium $50,000
    Male, $723; Female, $676
Premium $723 per year x 10 = $7,230
Cash surrender value of policy after 10 years = $6,450
Total dividends = $1,940
From $8,390 ($6,450 + $1,940) deduct the $7,230 and
    you get a profit of $1,160

You paid for the insurance, and you also realized a profit over the ten-year period. It looks like the insurance people might be right—and term insurance might have cost more. But what's wrong with this reasoning? Well, consider what you could have earned if you had taken $720 a year and put it in a savings account or invested it in blue chip stocks.

CHOOSING AMONG INSURANCE OPTIONS

Once you have decided on the type of insurance policy that is right for you, examine the various insurance options. Here are two options you are likely to run across:

1. *Giving the Company* the right to use the cash value of a policy to pay premiums that you have forgotten to pay is a pretty good option, particularly if you are careless. If you are prone to leaving envelopes unopened, if you don't heed warnings, if you take long vacations, or are slightly short of cash every once in a while, pick up this option. *It's free.*

2. *Paid-up insurance.* With paid-up insurance, all the premiums you are required to pay, from the time you take the policy to the time you die (provided that you live to be a hundred or less), are paid. It really is a pre-payment program. People elect this option because they fear that they will not have enough money to make the payments after their retirement. They are worried about having fixed expenses when they are old. For most people, however, the option is undesirable. Unless you have done almost no planning in your lifetime, you will need the policy for the death benefit less and less as you grow older. If you can't afford to keep up your insurance, it will probably happen in old age, the time when you will need it least. Meanwhile, you will have been paying for very expensive insurance at the highest possible premium rates, starting very early in life when you need the money to build your estate.

·15·

Small Gifts

To paraphrase the famed theatrical line, "There are no small gifts, only small financial plans." You have no need to fall into a tizzy when Aunt Mary or Uncle Sam puts twenty dollars in an envelope for your little boy's birthday. There are many wonderful investments you can make with that money. But the premier investment for your child is to get them into the stock market—with a DRIP!

DRIPS

No discussion of investing for children would be complete without mentioning DRIPs. DRIPs are dividend reinvestment programs, or stock ownership programs that you can enter into directly with companies like McDonald's, Kellogg's, and at least eight hundred more. Merely by calling or writing to these companies, you can get a list and a form for becoming part of their dividend reinvestment programs.

Once you are part of a DRIP you can invest small amounts of money that your children receive as gifts at parties, celebrations, or graduations. Perhaps you are the gift-giver, a grandma or grandpa, who likes to put away ten dollars a week for your grandchild. How do you buy something for them of real value? Well, you can buy a single share of stock in most of the major companies in this country. Most companies require you to buy at least a single share of stock before you can participate in their DRIP. You pay no brokerage commission, which could be substantial, when you're dealing with such small amounts of money. As the stock accumulates, the dividends, no matter how small, are reinvested to buy even a fraction of a share.

But, DRIPs can be used to invest large sums as well. You can put as much money as you like into a DRIP, purchasing several hundred shares. You are simply agreeing that as the stock pays dividends, all those dividends are reinvested into the same company. It's an ideal way to invest in stocks with very small amounts of money for children.

Some companies will even give you a discount on the market value of their stock. This discount can reach 30 percent of the value of the stock if it is traded on the stock exchange.

When I discussed DRIPs several years ago with my son, Arthur, then aged nine, he was really excited. He bought a share of stock in McDonald's, Burger King, and other companies that he thought enhanced his life. In his own book, *The Totally Awesome Money Book for Kids and Their Parents,* he'll tell you a lot about DRIPs. But more important, by using DRIPs, your children will learn about investing. Children introduced to DRIPs early on pretty quickly become experts in the stock market. It leads them to open up *The Wall Street Journal* (believe it or not) and check out how their share of stock is doing. Not only is a DRIP a money-making tool, it is a sophistication-builder.

Here are some actual small-gift situations and how you might wish to handle them.

Let's say that Grandma comes visiting with a fifty-dollar cash gift for your child. Fifty dollars is a perfect beginning for a DRIP. You can make your child a stockholder in McDonald's or Burger King.

Grandpa has come too, and he gifts $250. What do you do with it? You can contribute it to the DRIP as well, or you can lay the foundation for the child's mutual fund investing.

Putting small money into one or two stocks is an educational tool, but money diversified in a mutual fund over many, many years is a powerful wealth-building tool. Many funds accept a minimum amount of $250 to get started, while others require $1,000.

One fund especially created for children is the Scudder fund.

Let's say your child has accumulated $1,000 or even $3,000 at a confirmation, a bar mitzvah, or a graduation. What do you do with it? Here's my tip: You diversify into two or more mutual funds, one investing in small cap stocks, one investing in international stocks, and one investing in domestic value stocks. You leave the money there over a long period of time.

Suppose your daughter is sixteen years old, nearing college age, and has accumulated no money of her own. You've received $5,000 as a gift toward college tuition from Grandma and Grandpa. My suggestion is that you put it into your own money market account. Why? At this stage, she is very close to applying for financial aid. Thirty-five percent of any money she has will be counted as going toward tuition before any aid is given. But only 5 percent of the money you have accumulated is counted in your asset program before aid is awarded. So keep the money yourself, and keep it liquid. Do not invest it heavily because you have no time for the stock market to take its normal course with it. When the time comes for her to enter college, hand over to her whatever interest has grown in the intervening year or two.

Or let's say you can invest $100 for your son every month, not in a lump sum. What do you do? Here's my tip. If he is younger than seven, invest in mutual funds using what is called *dollar-cost averaging*. In dollar-cost averaging, you put the same amount of money every month into the same fund or variety of funds. That way you'll be buying at the highs and lows of the fund at random. Since most of the time the market is slightly low, you'll usually be buying low and later on selling high. That's the idea. Try to accumulate at least three funds: international, small cap, and a high-quality domestic equity fund.

Let's pretend interest rates have gone up. Do you buy income or interest investments for your daughter? Do you look into EE bonds, CDs, or perhaps a College Sure? If you have only a short period of time as she is ten years or older, it's a good idea to balance some of that high-growth equity investing with more typical traditional income-producing investments. Go back to your College Planning Worksheet in Chapter 11. There you can begin to see the direction you should go, depending on the age of your child.

·16·

Making Your Child a Successful Beneficiary

For some years I taught a course at the New School for Social Research in New York on "How to Be a Successful Beneficiary." The goal of the course was to guide a future beneficiary to knowledge of his expected inheritance and of how to incorporate it into his own financial plan. I learned how difficult it is to get children to ask about their inheritance rights, as they typically feel enormous restraint about raising the subject. Many families consider showing interest in a future inheritance to be greedy, morbid, or just plain impolite. As a result, children often walk on eggshells through adulthood and are not prepared to inherit.

Few parents *want* to sit down and tell a child the facts of money. There are some good reasons for such secretiveness. Parents want to feel free throughout their lives to spend, give away, or distribute their money as they wish. Personal finances are dynamic; they change all the time. But even if the amount of money in question remains the same, needs change, inflation takes its toll, and attitudes mature. And although the facts of life haven't changed in two million years, your money situation today may be different tomorrow. I assure you that a promise of money will fall upon your child's ears like a guarantee. Yet financial honesty and sharing are also important—at the right time and in the right place.

YOUR CHILD'S INHERITANCE RIGHTS

But your will must remain flexible throughout your life.

From the beginning you will want to know what your children's inheritance rights are so that you can manage them without the children's own involvement. What are inheritance rights of children?

If you die intestate (without a will), state law will be applied to your estate. Every state has a statute determining which of your heirs will inherit from you if you die intestate. This list changes from time to time as it is amended by the legislature of each state. By statute, these heirs are called your *distributees.*

For the most part, your state legislators are filled with good intentions. They suspect that you wish your spouse to inherit the most, followed by your children, then your remote relatives. You may have other ideas, however, in which case it is best to make a will.

Most states give approximately half of the estate to the children if one parent is surviving. Often a basic lump sum (for example, $25,000) is given to the surviving parent before the division into halves is made. If the estate amounts to less than this lump sum, the child will get nothing. But if no parent survives, the children usually share the estate equally among themselves. If you are survived by your spouse and several children, in many states your spouse will get a lump sum and only a third of the remainder; the children will share the other two-thirds equally. Often, if one of your children has predeceased you and left behind a child, your grandchild will take your child's share.

If a divorced parent remarries, in most states the second spouse will inherit more of the money or perhaps the entire estate over and above the child of the first marriage. If the parent has children from the second marriage, however, all the children from both marriages will likely inherit equally.

As you make your will, you can dictate the inheritance rights of your children, and your will will override the law's on intestacy. Many people believe that they are legally required to leave money to their children, but this is not true in most states.

Your will can be tailor-made for you. It can even include afterborn children, that is, children who have not yet been born at the time the will is made. If you are expecting an addition to your family, you may have already given thought to the inheritance of the unborn child. Merely by using the word *children* in the will, you will be including all children that you have (born or unborn, adoptive or natural) at the time of your death, except for illegitimate children.

Adoptive children have inheritance rights equal to those of natural children. If your will leaves property or money to "my children," the word *children* will include your adoptive children.

PARENTS' INHERITANCE RIGHTS

Because most children don't have money, very little thought is given to the rights of parents to inherit from the children. But parents, too, have inheritance rights. One young man I know is a millionaire (he is a computer game innovator), but his mother doesn't have much money. Another young man (a well-known film star) has enough wealth to, in the vernacular, "buy and sell his mom and dad." If your child is a ranking tennis pro or the creator of a new generation of computer software, you may be interested in the parental side of inheritance.

An adult son who is giving aid to his elderly mother may want to protect his mother in the remote event that he dies first. If he has no will, his legacy will be distributed in accordance with the laws of the state where the child resided at the time of his death. This may mean that the mother, as a remote relative (compared to his wife) gets nothing. If he left no widow, it is likely that the mother will inherit everything.

A child, however, can disinherit a parent just as a parent can disinherit a child. The child simply makes a will that leaves the money to others and not to the parent. The right to disinherit a parent is limited to adult children, since in most states people under the age of twenty-one cannot make a valid will. This restriction becomes unfortunate in some situations. An abusive parent may actually inherit from a child that he has abused. As a result, some states—

Connecticut being the most notable—have actually instituted divorce proceedings between parents and children. Either the parent or the child can initiate such proceedings. If it is successful, inheritance rights are cut off.

More usually, a severely abused child will become the subject of "termination of parental rights," a proceeding generally brought by a government agency, such as New York's Bureau of Child Welfare. A termination of parental rights nullifies any inheritance rights that the parent may have had from the child. The result can be a severing of all responsibilities of the child, who is then placed in a government or foster home and is available for adoption. If an adoption takes place, the adoptive parents take the inheritance rights. Sometimes a parent surrenders a child to a governmental agency and then an adoption takes place. Once new parents have been substituted in a legal adoption, no further relationship exists between the natural parent and the child, from a legal point of view. The adoptive parents have the right to inherit.

Parents of illegitimate children have rights that vary considerably from state to state.

Divorced parents retain their statutory rights to inherit from their children, regardless of the number of marriages. By the same token, both the children and the parent can disinherit each other. (See Chapter 18 for a discussion of inheritance rights as part of a separation agreement.)

MAKING A WILL

To avoid having the state government determine your children's inheritance rights, you simply make a will. You should make your will in the early stages of parenthood. There are

no excuses for failing to do this necessary task. It is estimated that only 10 percent of the American population has
wills. To me, this failure is tantamount to not voting. Having
a will is a great American right that you definitely should
exercise.

The three basic purposes of a will are:

1. To get your assets to the people you want to have them
2. To do your best tax planning
3. To pick the executors, trustees, and other fiduciaries
   who will administer your estate

Your Children as Beneficiaries

Assuming you make a will and you decide to include
your children as beneficiaries, you must determine whether
any of them are minors and whether they have any special
needs.

For all your children, your will should specify whether
they are to inherit *per capita* or *per stirpes*. Inheriting *per
capita* means that your money will be distributed equally
among all those individuals who stand in the same relation
to you. If one of them predeceases you, his share is divided
equally by the others. Inheriting *per stirpes* means that if
one of your children dies before you, his heirs—your grandchildren—divide up this share. Your grandchildren inherit
by right of their deceased parent. Here is an example of
each.

Per capita. Your three children are your beneficiaries
and are entitled to equal shares. Your son dies, so upon your
death your two daughters divide his share. Your son's own
two children get nothing.

Per stirpes. Your same three children are still your beneficiaries. Your son dies, and when you die, your two surviving daughters inherit their original share. Your son's share is divided equally between his children.

Your Grandchildren's Beneficiaries

Let's say one of your children has many children of his own, while your other children have only one each. You must first decide whether you want your grandchildren to inherit anything if their parents are still alive at the time of your death.

Once you have determined who your beneficiaries will be, consider what specific amounts you want to leave to each. You will have to decide whether you want the grandchildren with many brothers and sisters each to inherit less from you than the grandchildren who are only children.

The most difficult part of will-making when children are involved is deciding who your trustees and executors will be. The surviving parent is the most likely candidate to act in either capacity.

THE WILL'S PROVISIONS THAT AFFECT YOUR CHILDREN

Several will provisions particularly affect children and grandchildren. The following explanations of them may help you feel comfortable working with your attorney to prepare your will.

Leaving Personal Property

You may want your various children to receive specific items of your tangible personal property: jewelry, paintings, and the like. Specific stocks, bonds, and other cash substitutes may also be given. Sentiment will dictate your decisions. But the moving expenses, if any, related to the gift are the responsibility of the legatee, unless you specify otherwise, as are all liens against the property. Therefore, if you want your children to inherit your property free and clear, be sure they can afford to take it.

A specific legacy clause could read:

I give my gold pin with three emeralds to my daughter Nancy, if she survives me.

If your will specifies a certain piece of property to go to a specified legatee, you are not obligated to hold on to that property for the rest of your life. Many people who leave their gold earrings, say, think that they must change their will if they lose one of them or if they decide to cash them in because the price of gold has soared. Not so. If you die without owning that specific piece of property any longer, the legatee will simply not get anything. This is called *ademption,* or a *failed bequest.*

If you don't want the bequest to fail, you can state that in the event the personal property no longer exists, the legatee will get the dollar equivalent or another gift that you also specify.

There can be good reasons for leaving out specific bequests, particularly if you have more than one child. Perhaps you do not want all your children to know which of them is to get your retirement watch or your engagement ring. The alternative to announcing the facts in a will is the *letter precatory.* A letter precatory is a letter written in your own handwriting, signed by you, and given to your executor. It lists all the odds and ends of your personal property, both valuable and sentimental and who gets them, without publishing who gets them in the will. The executor, of course, must be someone you trust to carry out your wishes. I suggest that you do list very valuable items in the will. For sentimental items, don't clutter up your will but prepare a letter precatory.

Alternatively, your will can permit your executor, particularly if he or she is a spouse, to divide things up at his or her discretion. You could say, for example,

> *I leave my doll collection to my beloved daughters and I direct my husband John as executor to divide them among our daughters at his absolute discretion, having due regard for our daughters' preferences. John's decision shall be binding and conclusive.*

To make life easy for yourself, you can leave your personal property in a general way, like this:

> *I give, devise, and bequeath all of my jewelry, clothing, books, personal effects, household furnishings and equipment, automobiles, and other tangible personal property, wherever situate, which I own at the time of my death, together with my insurance policies, to my children, share and share alike.*

Leaving Money

You may wish to leave to your heirs, especially to your grandchildren, a specific amount of money. If you do, you can specify an amount of money to be from the cash available in your estate. If there is not enough cash at the time of your death, then only a part of that legacy, or perhaps none of it, will be paid.

Another way of giving money is by specifying a percentage of your estate rather than a specific amount of money. You may decide to give one-third or one-half of your estate to your heirs.

You can also make the gift flexible. For example, you can leave a stated sum, say $50,000, provided that the sum does not exceed five percent of your estate (and in the event that it does, the gift will be reduced to five percent). The remainder can be left to your more important heirs, such as your spouse and children.

In the type of legacy called the *demonstrative bequest,* you specify a certain amount of cash for someone and state where the cash is to be taken from. For example, you can state that your cousin is to get $10,000 out of a specific bank account. Your cousin will get the $10,000 if the bank account itself is still in existence but not necessarily if it is defunct, even if there is $10,000 elsewhere in the estate. In that case, the specific and general bequests are paid, then the demonstrative bequest is considered.

If you want to give stocks and bonds, pay attention to whether you are giving them as a specific bequest or as a demonstrative bequest. If you want your beneficiary to get a particular stock that you own at the time you make your will, then name the stock and put the certificate number right in the will. (You can still sell the stock; if you do, that beneficiary will simply not get it.) Otherwise, if you just leave a general disposition of AT&T stock, then it's possible that your executors will actually have to go out and buy some of that stock in the open market if none is in your estate. Remember, if you do give a specific stock, it carries with it any additional stock issued by the corporation after you have executed your will. (This might be in the form of a stock split in which a shareholder usually gets two shares of stock for every one they own at a value of half the original stock price for each of the new shares. The purpose is to increase the number of shares outstanding without changing the value. A corporation splits a stock when it is hot and they want to make it accessible to more people who want to buy it.)

A Typical Will Provision for a Minor Child

Typically, you will leave your minor child's share of your stock in trust with your surviving spouse or trustee. Similarly, you may create a trust for your grandchildren, naming their parents as trustees. Minors themselves (under eighteen or twenty-one, depending on the state in which they live) cannot act as executors or trustees. With a substantial trust, a professional trustee is preferable. (On selecting trustees, see Chapter 7.)

Children also receive bequests through a custodian when they reach a specified age. Contrary to what happens with a trust, no trustee is distributing income to the child's guardian during the period of minority. The bequest "vests" (belongs to the child) immediately, but the custodian controls the funds. If your child is to receive a share in a business or investment portfolio, you should designate a fiduciary, perhaps the executor, to manage those assets.

If, instead of making an outright gift, you create a trust, you must decide whether to create one single trust for all your children or a separate trust for each child. The consequences of each method are largely tax-related and administrative. Both methods can distribute income to the children at the trustee's discretion or, instead, provide for its accumulation. The principal can be invaded by the trustee for educational purposes or for emergencies. You can specify separate trusts that will terminate, distributing the funds to each of your heirs at a different date. You can also terminate a single trust at a specific date and have the assets be distributed to each child at a different time.

The single trust (often called a "pot" trust) is useful in a small estate, where bookkeeping for several trusts would be too expensive. Furthermore, if the trust income is small, the tax bracket will remain low, despite the lumping of all the bequests into one trust. On the other hand, with a large estate, separate trusts divide the funds among many children and create several low-income taxpayers.

Guardians

The appointment of a guardian to receive a minor's property is expensive and can be time-consuming. A wiser alternative in most cases is to give the executor power to hold and manage the property until the child reaches majority.

Disinheritance

Children can be disinherited, but the proper manner of doing so varies from state to state. In most states, making a will with no provision for your child is enough. Frequently, however, specific mention of disinheritance in the will is necessary to distinguish disinherited children from children born or adopted after the will was executed. Check with your attorney.

·17·

The Financial Rewards of Grandparenthood

Just when you thought you were ready to take your place in the sun, someone makes you a grandparent. It came out of nowhere. Your daughter, who you were sure would opt to become the first woman President of the United States, has twins instead. Your son, who you never expected would marry, marries and has a child within the first year.

This chapter deals with some special problems that come up in the financial planning of grandparents. If you are the parent of minor children as well as a grandparent, read everything twice. Good luck.

THE RIGHTS OF GRANDPARENTS

Grandparents have not only responsibilities but rights. For many years in this century, grandparents had no special rights with respect to their grandchildren. Parents were fully authorized to decide whether and when the grandparents would see their grandchildren. Presumably, the grandparents had enough control over their own children to get to see their grandchildren. The law was perfectly content to permit a family interchange based on the culture of the individual family. Most likely this situation would have remained if the divorce rate had not soared in the intervening years.

Divorce separates a mother and father into warring camps. It brings parents (especially mothers) back into the bosom of their former primary family (their own mom and dad). Often the grandparents on the side of the noncustodial parent were shut out from the family picture. Our custody laws place primary residential custody with the mother. The result was that unless the mother permitted the father's parents to see their grandchildren, they had very little right to do so.

Not only did divorce separate children from their father's parents; it sometimes separated them from their own parents, as well, such as when neither parent wished custody of the child, or when the state stepped in to separate the child from neglectful or abusive parents and put the child into foster care and, it is hoped, adoption. In other instances of increasing frequency, the parents were not legally married in the first place. The father may abandon the child, only to have the mother, unable to cope, disappear as well. Again, the state may step in. For some time, the natural parents had total authority and superior rights to the grandparents with respect to custody, visitation, and care of the child. Even the state in which the child resided had more authority than the grandparents. Grandparents were basically disposable assets in the American family.

Times have changed, largely for two reasons. First and foremost is the advent of the two-paycheck family. Working-class and middle-class parents now often hire their parents to baby-sit. (In most cases, I suggest payment to attain the hefty tax deduction available.) With the high cost of child care, baby-sitting grandparents may be the only way that both parents can work.

The second reason that grandparents are more fully in the picture these days is that they themselves have fought for their rights. Many grandparents have refused to permit the courts to determine the custody rights of their own grand-children without their being heard on the subject. Often they demand and obtain a court order insuring visitation rights. Not long ago, I was a guest on a call-in radio show on the subject of custody. Very few calls came in from parents. Instead, the majority were from children and grandparents. Grandparents, particularly those living in a different state from their grandchildren, were very concerned to gain the right to visit in the event of a divorce. They were concerned with whether the custodial parent (usually not their own child) would allow the grandchild to hop on a plane to visit them.

Once a custodial parent obstructs grandparents from seeing the child, families become polarized, and only very strong grandparents can remain neutral. The courts have slowly recognized the visitation rights and occasionally the custodial rights of grandparents. Today, thirty-four states permit grandparents to obtain court-ordered visitation rights.

The visitation rights of grandparents still vary from case to case, however. The best interest of the child applies. In some cases, particularly when the child lived with the grand-parents for a time, the court will find it in the best interest of the child to establish visitation rights. In other cases, the child would like to see the grandparents, but the court understandably prefers to deny the grandparents visitation rights rather than permit a visitation that could cause friction in the primary home. Custody expert Henry Foster writes, "The court will not interfere simply to better the moral and temporal welfare of the child as against an offending parent." In general, a parent who is not otherwise neglectful or abusive will not be ordered to permit visitation by the grandparents.

Custody proceedings can become more complex when a grandparent seeks custody from both the natural parents. Such a grandparent has a hard road to travel. In a contest between a parent and child, the best interest of the child would theoretically prevail, but in a contest between a parent and a nonparent, age-old considerations that go beyond the interest of the child apply. There, Foster comments, "No court should for any of the gravest reasons transfer the custody of the child from the natural parents to any other person." Parents have a superior right unless they are actually unfit to assume the duties of parenthood. Unlike in a custody fight between parents, merely showing where the child would be better off is not enough. Finding a better home, better surroundings, even people who are better equipped to care for the child, is insufficient. Instead, a grandparent must show a powerful unfitness and a real detriment on the part of the parent (or parents) in the event that custody is awarded to him (or them).

THE RESPONSIBILITIES OF GRANDPARENTS

The law imposes no financial responsibility upon grand-parents for grandchildren. Parents have an actual duty to support their natural child or their legally adopted child, but grandparents have no duty to support a grandchild. The buck stops with Mom and Dad. Therefore, the world of grandparental gift-giving, will-making, and other transfers is a voluntary world where grandparents are free to decide what they wish to do with their own funds.

It has happened that children of very wealthy parents will run away from home and give birth, and then go through a divorce. Regardless of the wealth of the parents, the parents have no legal responsibility to support their own child's progeny. In Canada, estranged or divorced custodial parents can sue the other partner's parents for support. But despite the law, many grandparents feel a moral responsi-bility to do so. Others go further and leave legacies to their grandchildren and even great-grandchildren.

Grandparents should keep this in mind as they read the next several sections. Their lack of legal obligations gives them both more and less financial advantage. Apart from emotional reasons, the major advantage of giving a contri-bution to a minor child is, again, tax savings. Because a grandparent may be in as low a tax bracket as a grandchild, there may be no difference in their bracket-rate ratios. On the other hand, as they are presumably closer to the end of life and therefore are coming up against estate-tax planning, they may find an overall estate-tax benefit in making gifts and transfers.

TAXES SEEN FROM GRANDPA'S VIEWPOINT

Many grandparents think of giving money to their minor grandchildren. (We will look only peripherally at financial planning between parents and their adult children since the same tax rules apply.)

As we examine the subject of gift-giving to grandchildren, we must concentrate on estate-tax savings over and above income-tax savings, the problems of gifting to grandchildren in different economic categories, control over the use of gifts without causing intrafamily problems, and grandparents' fear that the money will eventually be needed as they become older and perhaps ill.

In considering the transfer of money or other assets to grandchildren, grandparents should look at income taxes, estate taxes, and gift taxes.

For income taxes, always consider who will be taxed on the transferred property. The likelihood is that you will save on income taxes by transferring property to your grandchildren and that the income from that property will be taxed at their lower bracket and rate. If parents use income to satisfy a legal or support obligation, income tax may be applied to them at their higher tax bracket and rate. But since you are a grandparent and *do not have the legal obligation to support,* you will not run into this stumbling block.

When considering estate taxes, always look at whether the property will be subject to administration and be included in your gross estate or in your grandchild's gross estate. If you have relinquished ownership and control over the property and shifted the true ownership to your grandchildren, you will save on estate taxes. Again, unless the child predeceases.

I frequently advise clients not to make transfers merely because taxes will be saved. The worst thing that you can do is to transfer to a child funds that you may need, just to save eventual taxes. It makes no sense. For the most part, grandparents are conservative and do not willy-nilly give away their hard-earned money. But sometimes they experience a feeling of confusion and a conflict of goals. Planning for oneself is all well and good, but there is also a great deal of pleasure in providing for beloved grandchildren while you are still around to watch them enjoy it. Conflict can occur, too, when you have more than one grandchild with parents of very different economic standing. Love and money come into play here even more than in parent-child relationships.

For this reason, gift-giving by grandparents can be even more complex than parental giving. Parents are more likely to see the gift as a purely financial device, and all of their tax arrangements are geared toward permitting them to have their cake and eat it, too. Parents relinquish a certain degree of control over their money in return for various kinds of tax benefits, but they often feel that by giving money to a minor child, in trust or as a direct gift, it still belongs to them.

On the other hand, the grandparent sees a gift as actually gone. Even if the minor child has no control over the money, the parent or guardian will. The grandparent is often uncertain as to whether the gift is going for the benefit of the grandchild or the parent. Gifted money is often not spoken of and the grandparent is unsure as to its use and final distribution. The grandparent may be hesitant to stipulate how the money is to be spent for the grandchild. Looking over the parent's shoulder can result in friction rather than thanks. Grandparents may be concerned that their adult daughter will hand over to an irresponsible husband a gift they made to their grandchild. Of course, the father may be perfectly responsible but disapproved of by the grandparents, whose judgment determines how they give their own money.

Old Notions Can be Dangerous

Many grandparents have never planned financially. To them, everything that they will read in this book is new. If you used to be up on the facts about planning through gift-giving but no longer are, let me rid you of some out-of-date notions.

Prior to 1976, the law was completely different from what it is today. Back then you could give $3,000 per year per child without paying gift taxes. The rule was: "Many inter vivos gift transfers are motivated by a desire to reduce death taxes." Significant tax savings could be realized through inter vivos gifts. Gift-tax rates were only three-fourths of estate tax rates, so an inducement for lifetime gifts existed. Another tax-saving advantage was that the first gift made during your lifetime was taxed at the lowest marginal gift-tax rates. This favorable tax effect was another significant inducement to lifetime giving.

An additional inducement was that the gift tax paid was not included in your estate. As a result, significant transfer taxes on death could be saved by making lifetime transfers and paying one tax. Even a deathbed gift saved taxes. The amount of the deathbed gift would most likely be included in the gross estate, but the gross estate would not have included the amount of the gift tax paid on the deathbed transfer. By making the deathbed gifts, the transferor realized an estate-tax saving equal to the amount of the tax paid on the gift.

This situation changed in 1981 under the Economic Recovery Tax Act (ERTA). Older grandparents should know that a special provision, called "gross-up," enacted in 1981 provides that if a gift that is subject to gift tax is made within three years of death, the amount of the gift tax paid is included in the gross estate for estate-tax purposes, even though the gift is no longer part of the estate. So, any gift tax paid on any gift made by the deceased within three years of death, regardless of whether the property itself is included in the estate, becomes part of the gross estate. The ostensible purpose is to prevent transfer for the purpose of removing the gift-tax amount from the gross estate. It discourages last-minute gift-giving and gift-tax payments.

Removing the appreciation of property from the estate tax may also be on your mind. Another motivation for lifetime transfers to minor donees can be to remove the post-transfer income from, and appreciation of, the transferred property from the donor's tax base. Unification of the gift and estate taxes requires that adjusted taxable gifts be added to the taxable estate. Accordingly, the value of the gift at the date of death is included in the gross estate. Because date-of-gift value is used, any posttransfer appreciation in the value of the property is not subject to estate tax. This is a compelling motivation for making lifetime gifts. Donors who possess property that has significant growth potential, such as real estate or closely held stock, can achieve substantial transfer-tax savings by making lifetime transfers. Likewise, property with high income potential may be an appropriate gift.

If estate-tax consideration is what you have in mind, transferring a highly appreciated property such as your own home to a grandchild and continuing to keep a life estate for yourself (the right to live there for the rest of your life) can be a way of saving the home from sale in order to pay estate taxes. But keep the stepped-up basis strategies in mind. (See Chapter 2 for a discussion of stepped-up basis.)

Generation-Skipping Trusts

You may relinquish control over your money before your death but still wish to insure that this money continues to descend through the generations free of estate tax. To accomplish this "dynasty," it is necessary to create a "generation-skipping trust". Such a trust makes your child the beneficiary for life; upon his or her death, the trust belongs to your grandchildren.

During the lifetime of the first beneficiary (your adult child), under a GSK, both income and principal may be distributed periodically, thus assuring the beneficiary enough money to live on. At the death of the beneficiary, the money would go directly to your grandchildren. It is also possible to continue the trust beyond the grandchildren. The income from the trust may be further distributed during the lifetimes of the grandchildren, the great-grandchildren, the great-great-grandchildren, and so forth.

As a result, money has been permitted to pass tax-free through several generations. In 1976, with the imposition of a generation-skipping tax, a few trusts were restricted; most, however, are not. The following criteria render a trust subject to taxation:

1. The trust must have two or more beneficiaries.
2. At least two of the beneficiaries must be from different generations (for example, child and grandchild).
3. Each generation must be younger than that of the grantor (the one who establishes the trust).

The tax on these trusts is the same whether they are inter vivos (created in your lifetime) or testamentary (created in your will).

The following trusts are not subject to taxation:

1. Trusts to your children only
2. Trusts to your grandchildren only
3. Trusts to your spouse (that go to your child upon your spouse's death)
4. Generation-skipping trusts of less than $1 million

A special "exclusion" or "exemption" from this tax is available to grandparents. Transfers to grandchildren are not subject to the tax if the total transfer does not "exceed $1,000,000 per each transferor"—the grandparent's own child is considered the transferor.

Because of this high figure, most of you will be able to create a generation-skipping trust since most of you will not be giving more than $250,000 to each grandchild. Nevertheless, even if $30,000 or $40,000 is what you have in mind, you must be careful that your trust meets all the rules to be eligible for the grandchild exclusion. First of all, the property must actually be given to the grandchildren, so that if they die, it will become part of their own estate. If there are any contingencies regarding their going to school, getting married, or reaching a certain age before they can get the money, you will not get the exclusion unless they have actually already reached that age, performed that marriage, or fulfilled in some other way the stated contingency. If you have the financial wherewithal to be subject to a tax (you may want to transfer more than $1 million per transferor), the exclusion is applied the first time that a distribution is made to a grandchild. Make sure that your trustee understands this so that the first child to receive money does not use up all of the tax savings, leaving the other grandchildren to pay the tax.

The generation-skipping tax, when it is imposed, is an additional tax, separate from estate and gift tax. The tax will be paid not by the grantor but by the trust, based on the tax rate of the son or daughter. The tax is based upon the estate of the *deemed transferor*. That means that the child deemed to have made the transfer to his own child, not the grantor to the grandchildren. This makes it almost impossible for your children to prepare their own tax picture accurately. By leaving money to their children, you may be interfering with their estate plan. If you are in this situation, consider creating separate trusts for each generation rather than giving money for life to your own children and then to your grandchildren upon your children's death.

·18·

Gifting and Support Issues When Parents Divorce

A parent's legal obligation to support a child is a matter of state law, which varies from state to state. Depending on the state in which you reside, you must support your child until age eighteen or twenty-one, and the determination of which parent has the major financial responsibility differs. In most states, both parents, if they are able, have legal support obligations to their minor offspring.

While a marriage is going well, parents rarely think of their support obligation as a burden. But divorce often forces parents to focus on finances and to struggle with issues of who will support the child, who will have custody, and what the eventual relationship between parents and child will be. The posture that divorce puts many parents in is uncomfortable and alien to them.

Still, the average divorcing couple today will consist of a wife-mother with custody of the child and a husband-father with support obligations. The parents, once an economic team, are now at economic odds. What was good for one financially used to be good for both, but often in divorce every dollar that the father is not obligated to pay to the mother for support inures to his benefit alone. The mother and children may become a burden to a once-devoted husband and father.

Confusion and often anger are the norm. A mother who has custody is often nervous about asking the father for enough money to live comfortably. Frequently, her goal is merely to make ends meet, but even then she may be concerned that support will be insufficient . The father may be concerned that his ex-wife will turn the child against him while he is paying the freight. He will also consider his personal freedom and whether he will be able to seek a new relationship and offer financial security to a new wife and future children. It may be that neither the husband nor the wife has previously focused on his or her personal finances or taken any steps toward financial control.

WHAT WILL THE COURT DECIDE?

What both sides really want to know is what the court will do. What will happen if the parents cannot agree on the father's legal obligation to support? What obligations will the judge impose? Any attorney who does not want to mislead a client will generally say that a support award is unpredictable and that settlement is the best course. There are some rules of thumb and there are some criteria.

Without a doubt, it is best if both parties can agree upon their legal obligations. Understanding that point is already knowing a great deal about your legal obligations to your children. First and foremost, you have an obligation to make sure that your children thrive. If you do not, you are a neglectful parent, and in extreme cases your parental rights can be terminated and the child can be removed from your care.

But beyond this very basic obligation to feed, clothe, house, and educate the child, there are no hard and fast rules. That is why an intact family rarely brushes with the concept of support obligation. Our government hardly ever looks over the shoulders of married parents. On the contrary, we would consider it the utmost breach of freedom if our government dictated to us the kind of clothing, toys, television, and books that we were to give our children. Yet in a divorce setting, parents must think about these things for the first time, because one party (usually the mother) will be making the decisions regarding the child and the other party (usually the father) will be paying for them.

It is only natural for Mom to want to know what she can expect in terms of funds and for Dad to protect his control over important decisions. The law gives them the freedom to contract and make joint decisions. There are no rules regarding how much support a child should have at any age. Instead, the court will look at several factors in making an award of support:

- the age of the child
- any special needs of the child (medical, educational)
- the income and assets of both parents

- the potential of both parents' future income
- the child's current lifestyle (to provide continuity despite the divorce)
- the child's own assets, if any

Once the court considers these factors, it applies the law of the state regarding who has responsibility for child support. Not so long ago, only the father had financial responsibility for the child, but this is no longer the case. In May 1980, a man from Alabama claimed that the divorce law of Alabama was unconstitutional because it discriminated against him on the basis of sex. He argued that because the court could award support only to a mother and not to a father, the law was unconstitutional. His case was taken to the Supreme Court of the United States, which rarely hears domestic relations cases. The court found the Alabama law unconstitutional. Interestingly, it did not hold that sex discrimination against the male was at issue. Rather, it held that by making support obligations go only from the male to the female, the law recognized the female's dependency; in the long run, the female would experience discrimination in the job market because of the underlying belief that she would be taken care of by her man.

The effect of the Supreme Court decision was to make our domestic relations laws nationwide "gender neutral," though in many states there was already an obligation on the part of a mother, whether or not she was the custodian, to provide for the child.

Once responsibility is assigned, the court may award support in an unallocated fashion. In other words, an amount of weekly or monthly payments will be granted without distinguishing how much goes for the support of the dependent spouse (often the wife) and how much for the child's support. In determining the amount, there are few rules of thumb.

One very important rule, however, is that courts will rarely make an award requiring one party to pay to another party more than half of his salary. The reason is evident: A court does not wish to eliminate the incentive to work and earn. When so little of the salary is kept, there is great danger that the supporting spouse (usually the husband) will disappear.

To avoid uncertainty, many couples are prepared to make their own decisions and to translate them into the terms of a signed separation agreement. In most states, these agreements will be incorporated into a future divorce decree and will be as binding upon the couple as if a judge had made the decision for them. In some states, the separation agreement plus living apart are sufficient grounds for divorce and can be converted into a divorce after the parties have lived separately for the period of time specified by state law. Most important to the couple as parents, the separation agreement will memorialize their legal obligations to their child until the child reaches the age of majority and, in certain cases, beyond.

A REASONABLE APPROACH TO CHILD SUPPORT

In order to sort out a reasonable approach to child support, you as a divorcing parent may make certain decisions about what you want in the privacy of your home before speaking to an attorney. These points should be reviewed from time to time as negotiation progresses.

Identify Key Issues in Child Support

First, decide on all of the issues that you wish to focus on in determining child support. Here is a list that I use in my office that I believe covers the fundamental needs.

- Custody: joint, sole, split (the child lives with each parent part time)
- Future residence
- Visitation schedule
- Notification if visiting parent can't make it
- Notification of child's whereabouts
- Free access to child
- Fostering affection
- Child's surname
- Religious upbringing
- Decision-making with regard to health care and education
- Medical and dental costs; insurance
- Educational costs, now and in college
- Trips, entertainment, camp, and equipment
- Clothing

Check this list against your final agreement to be sure you have considered all of them.

Prepare a Budget that Covers the Child's Needs

Second, prepare a budget to cover the needs of the child alone. (Those of you who have prepared a pay-yourself-first budget know what I mean.) In a divorce proceeding, you will be required to prepare a budget for the court or for your attorney; each state has its required forms. I prefer to add a rider that projects the child's expenses to the time of majority.

This budget is usually prepared by the dependent custodial parent. Because divorce generally takes place in an adversarial setting, the custodial parent is often perceived as the defender or champion of the child, with the responsibility for fighting for every penny against a highly resistant, uncaring, noncustodial parent. Instead, I suggest that both parents independently create a budget for the child's future needs. The likelihood is that they will have substantial agreement on present needs but great disparity on what they would like to do for the child in the future.

Orthodontia, summer camp, trips, and, of course, college and postgraduate education are the usual future expenses that frighten the supporting parent. The custodial parent may see any refusal to provide for these items as a clear indication that the noncustodial parent no longer cares for the child and has disassociated himself from the family. This is not necessarily true. These major expenses may meet with resistance for other reasons: They may simply be too costly, or the uncertainty of future costs may disturb the noncustodial parent. Often, he simply does not want to be pushed around. To alleviate that problem, most attorneys are expert in drafting clauses that give the noncustodial parent the right to be consulted and sometimes even to make a final decision on things like education, health, and other important and expensive items.

Frequently, in order to give the noncustodial parent a

fair amount of control, payments may be made directly to the child rather than to the custodial parent—in the form of an allowance—or directly to the school, doctor, or summer camp. These are areas of negotiation. When the tendency is for the custodial parent to want all of the money and all of the decision-making power and the noncustodial parent, all of the decision making power and no dollar figure to which he or she is obligated, the result is a court-ordered award.

Make Provisions for Education

In deciding on payments for education, a lot will depend on whether the family has already provided for the child's education. Usually it hasn't. If a court believes that a child is capable of going to school and profiting by it, and if the financial station of the family is such that they would ordinarily be expected to provide for the child, it may order one or both parents to provide for a child's college education. (It will rarely order postgraduate or professional school payments.) I have seen such obligations imposed when the child is quite young. Years later, however, when the child is ready for school and the noncustodial parent is called upon to provide for education, he or she may not have the money. As in the case of the intact family that never saved for college, it is too late for these parents to obtain the funds.

Many divorced parents refuse to fill out financial-aid forms. They are fearful of disclosing their income and assets because they are concerned that the ex-spouse will try to reopen the case. Other noncustodial parents have simply grown so far apart from their children that they don't care enough to fill out the forms. Much needless anger and heartbreak can result even from the mere refusal to cooperate, let alone to contribute toward the payment of college costs.

The moral is, that having a clause in the agreement regarding college is not enough. The agreement should also include some form of college-savings program (see Chapter 12) to assure the existence of funds. Perhaps a trust is the answer, since it can be monitored by the custodial parent over the years. Another possibility is tuition-plan insurance. (See Chapter 13.) While I do not suggest this for the intact family, it is a way of enforcing college payments for divorcing parents.

In general, the key to providing for college education and other needs in a separation agreement is to make it practical.

Protect Your Child's Inheritance

Most states do not require you to leave your money to your child. While many states do require a spouse to provide at least one-third of the estate to the surviving mate, a child can be disinherited completely. A custodial parent may insist that the noncustodial parent make a will leaving money to the couple's child. If so, the parent is insisting on more rights than the child would have if the couple remained together.

There is an understandable tendency to believe that a divorced parent is more likely to disinherit the child than a parent in an intact family. Yet it has been my experience that few noncustodial parents insist that the custodial parent make a will leaving a portion of his estate to the child. But in this, as in other divorce matters, it should not be assumed that only the noncustodial parent needs to be monitored. The custodial parent may have a substantial estate, for example. There is nothing wrong with having a mutual agreement to make a will giving certain rights of inheritance to the child or children of the first marriage.

Sometimes an important asset, like the marital home or a second home, can be divided by agreement only if the parties are sure that it will be left to the children of the first marriage.

A particular case comes to mind in which a divorcing English couple were spending a great deal of time discussing the family silver, which had been in one or the other's family for centuries. Finally, they agreed to divide up the silver but to prepare a *contractual will* leaving the silver to the children as each of the parties died. Contractual wills are separate wills accompanied by a binding contract prohibiting change without the consent and knowledge of the other.

THE TAX CONSEQUENCES OF DIVORCE

In 1984, Congress made sweeping changes in the tax law affecting domestic relations, all of them becoming effective by January 1, 1985. In the following discussion, these changes have been taken into account.

In evaluating the tax consequences of your divorce and support agreements, you should concentrate on three questions:

1. What taxes will you pay on periodic payments, or if you are the supporting parent, what will you deduct?
2. What child-related income tax deductions will you get as opposed to your former spouse?
3. Who will take the exemption?

If a court makes an award, it is obligated to take the tax consequences of a support payment into consideration. The tax consequences are a matter of federal law. The rules are simple:

Support for a former spouse.

Support for a former spouse is taxable to the custodial parent and deductible from the gross income of the supporting parent. To qualify as alimony, the payments must be made in cash, and the court order or separation agreement must state that the payments will terminate at the recipient's death. Any deductible payments over $10,000 a year must continue for at least six years and should not decrease by more than $10,000 a year. If they do decrease by more than $10,000 in any of the first six years, the alimony is subject to recomputation, with the effect being that part of the alimony deduction will be denied. Spouses can agree to designate the payments as direct payments of expenses or nonperiodic payments instead of alimony.

Child Support.

By contrast, child support is not included in the taxable income of the recipient, nor is it deductible by the provider.

Other Monies.

Unallocated support (not specifically alimony or child support) will be treated as alimony unless any payments are reduced due to a contingency relating to a child, such as attaining a certain age, dying, or leaving school. To the extent that they are reduced, the payments are treated as child support and not alimony. Any contingency clearly associated with a child, such as payments that terminate in the same month as a child's eighteenth birthday, would have the same effect. Remember, no inclusion or deductions take place unless the payments are made pursuant to a court order or separation agreement. (Money given informally is neither taxable nor deductible.)

Property Transfer.

Property settlements are neither included as income by the recipient nor deducted by the transferor. Transfers of property between spouses incident to a divorce are tax-free. The basis of the property in the hands of the recipient will be the same as the transferor's.

Exemptions.

Who gets the exemption is also a matter of federal law. As a couple, you can agree and even alternate with regard to exemptions. If you say nothing in your agreement, then the custodial parent gets the exemption as long as more than half the child's support comes from the parents. The noncustodial parent will get the exemption only if the custodial parent signs a written statement allowing the noncustodial parent to claim the exemption. This statement must be attached to the noncustodial parent's tax return.

Child-related deductions as described in Chapter 17 are a matter of who pays for what. However, their distribution can be agreed upon by the parents.

ALIMONY TRUSTS

Alimony trusts can take the guesswork and anxiety out of support payments, and they are useful in other respects as well.

By *alimony trust*, I mean a support trust—a trust created

by a supporting parent in lieu of making periodic payments directly. The income from such a trust is paid to the custodial parent in satisfaction of the noncustodial parent's legal obligation to provide support. Upon the death or remarriage of the custodial parent, the principal goes to the child or another beneficiary as remainderman. The trust is created as part of a separation agreement or a writing in itself referred to in the agreement, and the terms are incorporated into a subsequent divorce decree.

This type of trust is governed by the Internal Revenue Code Section 682, which provides that the income from the trust be included in the custodial parent's gross income; this parent is considered the beneficiary of the trust, and that the income received is taxed to him directly.

Note that for this type of trust there must already be a legal separation or divorce. On the other hand, Section 682 does not *require* that the trust itself be *created* to discharge the legal obligations of the supporting parent or because of any family or marital relationship. It merely requires a trust, a divorce or legal separation, and income distributed to one parent. The trust may have been created before or after the divorce and for any purpose whatsoever.

In fact, it is never too late to create an alimony trust. The same tax and planning consequences can result if a trust is created subsequent to a divorce or separation, as long as under Section 682 monies are received by the custodial parent incident to a settlement and an existing decree is amended to include reference to the trust or amended agreement in which the trust is created.

Effect on Other Deductions
Charitable, medical, and standard deductions must be

considered in weighing the consequences of direct versus trust payments in any given case. For example, medical expenses may be deducted only if they are in excess of three percent of adjusted gross income. If income were excluded because a trust was created, the noncustodial parent could meet the three percent test more easily than if income were included to arrive at adjusted gross income and only then deducted as direct support.

Charitable contributions may be taken only up to 50 percent of adjusted gross income (20 percent for certain charities). Therefore, in contrast to medical expenses, a higher adjusted gross income is desirable. Here, direct payments leaving the adjusted gross income undiminished are more favorable.

Income from investment of funds that could otherwise be used as trust corpus may preclude the use of a standard deduction. For the noncustodial parent–taxpayer with few itemized deductions, a trust permitting gross income to be minimized can be very useful.

Overview

Alimony trusts are useful, then, to:

- give the noncustodial parent control over funds while providing income to the custodial parent
- give the custodial parent security
- remove income taxation from the noncustodial parent and transfer the entire income to the custodial parent
- avoid dissolution of income-producing assets
- provide a custodial parent with a distributive share of the family wealth.

HOW TO MAKE VOLUNTARY PAYMENTS TO CHILDREN WITH NO STRINGS ATTACHED

Too often, I have seen devoted fathers decline to pay for summer camp, buy a special piece of clothing, or even give an elaborate Christmas gift, for fear that this will open the door to the mother's claim that the father has more money than he is giving out. With equal frequency, I have seen fathers give elaborate gifts to a child and not make the mundane monthly payments to the mother. They may feel that making a showy display will do more to gain his child's love than putting food on the table.

In either case, help is available through use of the *voluntary payment clause* in divorce decrees or separation agreements. This clause permits either parent to make payments for the child without further payments being considered a legal obligation, without the payment or gift becoming evidence of an ability to pay more, and without diminishing the custodial parent's right to go after enforcement of other clauses in the agreement.

Appendix A
Your Child's Tax

DO YOU HAVE TO USE FORM 8615 TO FIGURE YOUR CHILD'S TAX?

Start Here

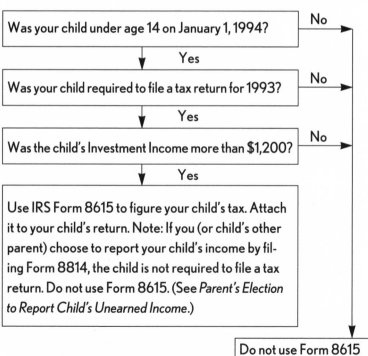

Was your child under age 14 on January 1, 1994? — No →

Yes ↓

Was your child required to file a tax return for 1993? — No →

Yes ↓

Was the child's Investment Income more than $1,200? — No →

Yes ↓

Use IRS Form 8615 to figure your child's tax. Attach it to your child's return. Note: If you (or child's other parent) choose to report your child's income by filing Form 8814, the child is not required to file a tax return. Do not use Form 8615. (See *Parent's Election to Report Child's Unearned Income.*)

Do not use Form 8615 to figure your child's tax.

CAN YOU INCLUDE YOUR CHILD'S INCOME ON YOUR TAX RETURN?

Start Here

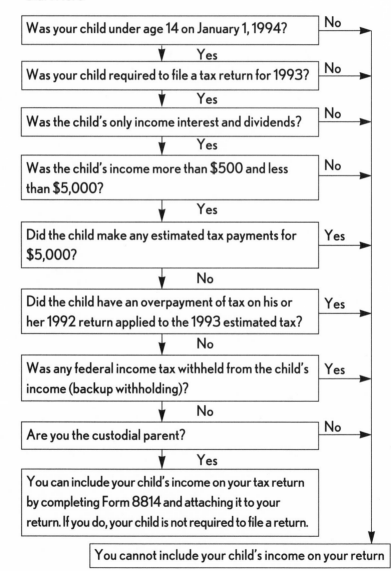

Was your child under age 14 on January 1, 1994? — No →

↓ Yes

Was your child required to file a tax return for 1993? — No →

↓ Yes

Was the child's only income interest and dividends? — No →

↓ Yes

Was the child's income more than $500 and less than $5,000? — No →

↓ Yes

Did the child make any estimated tax payments for $5,000? — Yes →

↓ No

Did the child have an overpayment of tax on his or her 1992 return applied to the 1993 estimated tax? — Yes →

↓ No

Was any federal income tax withheld from the child's income (backup withholding)? — Yes →

↓ No

Are you the custodial parent? — No →

↓ Yes

You can include your child's income on your tax return by completing Form 8814 and attaching it to your return. If you do, your child is not required to file a return.

You cannot include your child's income on your return

Appendix B
Children's Trust Agreement

Agreement made and entered into this ____ day of November, 199 ___ by and between:

Father, residing at _____
New York, hereinafter called the "Grantor"; and

Grandfather, residing at _____
and Friend with offices located at _____,
hereinafter called the "Trustees."

1. *Trust Property:* The Grantor hereby transfers and delivers to the Trustee the property described in Schedule A attached hereto and made a part hereof, and the Trustee agrees to hold that property and all additions thereto and the income therefrom upon the terms and conditions hereinafter set forth. Additional property may from time to time be transferred by the Grantor or by any other person or persons to the Trustee with his consent, and that property shall become a part of the trust property and shall be held, managed, invested, reinvested, and disposed of on the same terms and conditions as the property described in Schedule A;

2. *Dispositive Provisions:* The Trustee shall hold, manage, invest, and reinvest the trust property for the sole benefit of _____
("Beneficiary") child of the Grantor, upon the following terms:

a. The Trustee may distribute to, or apply for the sole benefit of, the Beneficiary until he attains the age of twenty-one (21) years so much of the income and principal, and at such times and in such amounts and manner as the Trustee may, in his discretion, deem reasonably necessary for the proper care, support, maintenance, or education of the Beneficiary. Any amount of income that the Trustee shall determine not to use may be accumulated and added to the principal;

b. When the Beneficiary attains the age of twenty-one (21) years, this trust shall terminate and the entire trust property then remaining shall be paid over and distributed to him, free and discharged of all trust;

c. Should the Beneficiary die before attaining the age of twenty-one (21) years, this trust shall terminate and the entire trust property then remaining shall be paid over and distributed to such persons in such shares and in such manner as the Beneficiary may appoint by his last Will, provided that this power of appointment is specifically referred to in the Will.

d. Should the Beneficiary die before attaining the age of twenty-one (21) years, without validly exercising the general testamentary power of appointment referred to in the previous paragraph, the Trustee shall pay over and distribute the entire trust property then remaining to the then-surviving issue of the Grantor in equal shares per stirpes, or, if there is no issue of the Grantor then surviving, to the person or persons who shall be appointed to administer the estate of the Beneficiary, to be disposed of as a part of that estate. In the event that a trust is established for such surviving issue of the Grantor, such trust property shall be added to such trust and administered as part thereof.

3. *Spendthrift Provision:* The interest of the Beneficiary in the income or principal of this Trust shall be free from control or interference of

any creditor or the spouse of the Beneficiary and shall not be subject to attachment or susceptible of alienation;

4. *Trustee's Powers:* The Trustee shall have all the powers and authority that are now or may hereafter be conferred by law upon him. In addition, he shall have in the administration of the Trust, full power and authority to:

a. Hold, manage, maintain, improve, preserve, and control all of the property in the Trust, collect and receive all dividends, interest, rent and other income thereof, and pay all taxes, expenses, costs, charges, claims, demands, and liabilities imposed upon, incurred, or arising in connection with the Trust, the property therein, and the administration and management thereof in such manner as he may, in his sole discretion, deem advisable;

b. Purchase and invest and reinvest the trust funds in, and sell, change and exchange, such stocks, bonds, other investments, or property, real or personal, as he may, in his sole discretion, deem advisable, including participation in any common trust fund established and maintained for the collective investment of fiduciary funds, as long as such funds are lawful investments authorized by the State of New York for fiduciaries. Any sale or other disposition of any property may be for cash or upon such terms of credit or otherwise as the Trustee may, in his sole discretion, deem advisable. No purchaser or purchasers or property from the Trustee hereinabove shall have any duty to see to the application of the purchase money;

c. Hold and retain any of the property coming into his hands hereunder in the same form as that in which the property shall have been received, without liability for loss or depreciation resulting from such retention.

d. Take, hold, or transfer any of the securities, bonds, or other property in the trust in his name as Trustee of the said trust.

e. Transfer or exchange any property held in trust, at any time, at such prices upon such terms and conditions, as he, in such manner as he may, in his sole discretion deem advisable;

f. Determine in cases of doubt whether money or property coming into its possession shall be treated as principal or income or apportioned between principal and income, and charge or apportion expenses, losses, and taxes either on income or on property to principal or income, as he may, in his sole discretion, deem proper;

g. Exercise all rights with respect to any stocks, bonds, other securities, or real or personal property held by him, and all persons, firms, and corporations are authorized to deal with the Trustee in connection with the securities or property as if he is the sole owner thereof;

h. Employ or consult with whatever agents, advisors, and legal counsel he may, in his sole discretion, deem advisable in connection with his duties hereunder, and determine and pay to these persons, firms, or corporations the reasonable value of his services;

i. Compromise and adjust any and all claims in favor of or against the trust upon such terms as he may, in his sole discretion, deem advisable.

j. Make, execute, and deliver all contracts, deeds, assignments, powers, other instruments, and, in general, any and all things for the preservation and management of the trust that he may, in his sole discretion, deem advisable;

k. Notwithstanding the preceding provisions of this Section 4, decisions by the Trustee as to what is income and what is principal, whether to charge or credit income, principal, or both, with expense, gains, losses, premiums, discounts, waste, or appreciation or depreciation in value, whether to establish sinking funds for taxes, assessments, insurance premiums, repairs, improvements, depreciation, or obsolescence, and all similar questions shall be made on the basis of the law of the State of New York, provided that if the law of New York on any such question has not been established or is unclear, the

Trustee may decide that question in such manner as he deems just, and his decision shall then bind all interested parties;

5. *Limitation on Powers:* Notwithstanding the provisions of Section 4, none of the powers accorded the Trustee shall be construed to enable the Grantor, the Trustee, or any other person to purchase, exchange, or otherwise deal with or dispose of the principal or income of this trust for less than an adequate or full consideration in money or money's worth, or to enable the Grantor, any corporation, or other entity in which the Grantor has a substantial interest, or the Trustee to borrow the principal of this trust, directly or indirectly, without adequate interest or security. No person other than the Trustee shall have or exercise the power to vote or direct the voting of any corporate shares or other securities of this trust; to control the investment of this trust, either by directing investments or reinvestment or by vetoing proposed investments or reinvestment; or to reacquire or exchange any property of this trust by substituting other property of an equivalent value.

6. *Provisions Regarding Trustee:* In addition to provisions applicable to Trustee generally, the following provisions shall apply to the Trustee:

a. No bond or surety shall be required of the Trustee or of any Successor Trustee who shall serve hereunder.

b. The Trustee or any Successor Trustee may resign by an instrument in writing;

c. The Trustee may appoint any person, firm, or corporation to serve as Successor Trustee;

d. In the event of death, resignation, or incapacity of _____, then in such event _____ is hereby appointed as Successor Trustee;

e. Any Successor Trustee shall have and may exercise all the rights, power, duties, and discretion conferred or imposed on the Trustee;

f. No Successor Trustee shall be responsible in any way for

any acts or omissions of any previous Trustee;

    g. No Trustee shall be liable for any act or omission, unless it is due to the Trustee's own willful default;

7. *Payments to Beneficiary:* During the minority of the Beneficiary, the Trustee may make any payments hereunder directly to the Beneficiary, to the guardian of the Beneficiary's person, to any other person deemed suitable by the Trustee, or for his expenses;

8. *Irrevocability:* This Trust is irrevocable, and the Grantor shall have no right whatsoever to alter, amend, revoke, or terminate this Trust in whole or in part. By this Trust Agreement, the Grantor intends to and does hereby relinquish absolutely all possession and enjoyment of the right to income from the trust property, as well as all right to designate the persons who shall possess or enjoy the trust property or the income therefrom, and the Grantor shall have the right at any time to release, renounce, or disclaim any interest whatsoever that might be construed to defeat his intention. Neither the creation of this trust nor any distribution of any income or principal thereof shall be deemed or considered to discharge or relieve the Grantor from his obligation to support any dependent.

9. *Situs:* This Trust shall be construed and regulated according to the laws of the State of New York;

10. *Counterparts:* This Agreement shall be executed in several counterparts, each one of which shall be deemed to be an original though the others be not produced.

    In witness whereof, the parties hereto have signed this Agreement on the date first above written.

_____
Grantor

_____
Trustee

_____
Trustee

Appendix C
Certificate of the Jones Family
Limited Partnership
(Sample)

This Certificate is executed on November ____, 199_, with respect to the agreement of The Jones Family Limited Partnership ("the Partnership").

1. *Name.* The Partnership's name is The Jones Family Limited Partnership.

2. *Partnership's Business.* The Partnership's business is all lawful acts of a Partnership under the Laws of the State of New Jersey.

3. *Registered Agent.* The name and post office address of the Partnership's agent is:

James Jones
1235 Elm Street
West Orange, NJ 07052

Mr. Jones is the sole general partner (General Partner). He resides and has his business address within the State of New Jersey.

4. *Specified Office.* The post office address of the office at which its records are kept is:

Mr. James Jones
1235 Elm Street
West Orange, NJ 07052

5. *Partners.* The name and post office of the General Partner is:

James Jones
1235 Elm Street
West Orange, NJ 07052

6. *Dissolution.* The latest date on which the Partnership is to be dissolved and its affairs wound up is _____ .

In witness whereof, the undersigned sole General Partner has signed and sealed this Certificate, on the day and year first above written.

_____
James Jones, General Partner

Appendix D
Power of Attorney

Notice: This is an important document. Before signing this document, you should know these important facts. The purpose of this Power of Attorney is to give the person whom you designate (your "Agent") broad powers to handle your property, which may include powers to pledge, sell, or otherwise dispose of any real or personal property without advance notice to you or approval by you. You may specify that these powers will exist even after you become disabled, incapacitated, or incompetent. The powers that you give your Agent are explained more fully in New York General Obligations Law, Article 5, Title 15, Sections 5-1502A through 5-1503, which expressly permits the use of any other or different form of Power of Attorney desired by the parties concerned. This document does not authorize anyone to make medical or other health care decisions for you. If there is anything about this form that you do not understand, you should ask a lawyer to explain it to you.

Know Everyone by These Presents, which are intended to constitute a General Power of Attorney pursuant to Article 5, Title 15 of the New York General Obligations Law:

That I _____ ("Principal"), residing at

_____, do hereby appoint:

_____

residing at

_____

(If two or more persons are to be appointed Agents with each Agent to be able to act ALONE without requiring the consent of any other Agent appointed in order to act, insert the name and address of each Agent SEPARATELY appointed and BE SURE TO insert the word "OR" between EACH designation of an Agent to show that EACH Agent has COMPLETE power to act alone.)

(If two or more persons are to be appointed Agents to act TO-GETHER and requiring the JOINT consent of ALL Agents JOINTLY appointed, BE SURE TO insert the word "AND" between EVERY DESIGNATION of each Agent to designate that ALL Agents listed are required to act together and NONE can act alone.)

My Attorney(s)-in-fact to act _____ .

(If more than one Agent is designated and the Principal wants each Agent alone to be able to exercise the power conferred, insert in this blank the word "JOINTLY.")

(The failure to make any insertion in this blank will require the Agents to act either separately or jointly, in accordance with the Principal's use of the word "OR" or the other word "AND" between every respective designation of such Agents above. If the Principal's wishes cannot be determined because he fails to insert the word "OR," "AND," "SEPAR-ATELY," or "JOINTLY" as he is asked to do above, the Principal will be deemed to require the Agents designated above to act jointly.)

IN MY NAME, PLACE, AND STEAD in any way, which I myself could do, if I were personally present, with respect to the following matters as each of them is defined in Title 15 of Article 5 of the New York General Obligations Law to the extent that I am permitted by law to act through an Agent:

Initial in the box any one or more of the
subdivisions as to which the Principal WANTS
to give the Agent authority.

[NOTICE: The Principal must write his or her initials in the corresponding blank space of a box below with respect to each of the subdivisions (A) through (N) below for which the Principal WANTS to give the Agent(s) authority. If the blank space within a box for any particular subdivision is NOT initialed, NO AUTHORITY WILL BE GRANTED for matters that are included in that subdivision.]

(A) real estate transactions; .... [   ]
(B) chattel and goods transactions; .... [   ]
(C) bond, share, and commodity transactions; .... [   ]
(D) banking transactions; .... [   ]
(E) business operating transactions; .... [   ]
(F) insurance transactions; .... [   ]
(G) estate transactions; .... [   ]
(H) claims and litigation; .... [   ]
(I) personal relationships and affairs; .... [   ]
(J) benefits from military service; .... [   ]
(K) records, reports, and statements; .... [   ]
(L) full and unqualified authority to my attorney(s)-in-fact to
     delegate any or all of the foregoing powers to any person
     or persons whom my attorney(s)-in-fact shall select; .... [   ]
(M) all other matters; .... [   ]

(N) if the blank space in the box to the right is initialized by the
  Principal, this Power of Attorney shall not be affected by the
  subsequent disability or incompetence of the Principal;... [   ]

(Special provisions and limitations may be included in the statutory
short form Power of Attorney only if they conform to the requirements
of Section 5-1503 of the New York General Obligations Law.)

This Power of Attorney shall not be affected by the subsequent disability of the Principal, it being intended that this Power of Attorney
shall be a Durable Power of Attorney.

To induce any third party to act hereunder, I hereby agree that any
third party receiving a duly executed copy or facsimile of this instrument may act hereunder, and that revocation or termination hereof
shall be ineffective as to such third party unless and until actual notice
or knowledge of such revocation or termination shall have been
received by such third party, and I for myself and for my heirs, executors, legal representatives, and assigns, hereby agree to indemnify
and hold harmless any such third party from and against any and all
claims that may arise against such third party by reason of such third
party having relied on the provisions of this instrument.

In Witness Whereof, I have hereunto signed my name and affixed my
seal on _____ .

_____
            (name, seal)
        (Signature of Principal)

Appendix E
Acknowledgments
for Wills and Trusts
(Sample)

State of New York: County of New York (month, date, year)

On April 25, 1996, before me personally came John Jones, to me known, and known to me to be the individual described in, and who executed the foregoing instrument and acknowledged to me that he executed the same.

William K. Notary

Affidavit as to Power of Attorney being in full force
State of New York: County of New York (month, date, year)

Arthur Smith, being duly sworn, deposes and says that John Jones, as Principal, who resides at 100 Fifth Avenue, New York, NY 10007 did, in writing, under date of April 25, 1996, appoint me his true and lawful attorney, and that annexed thereto, and hereby made a part hereof, is a true copy of said Power of Attorney.

That, as attorney-in-fact of said Principal and under and by virtue of the said Power of Attorney, I have this day executed the following described instrument.

That, at the time of executing the above-described document instrument, I had no actual knowledge or actual notice of revocation or termination of the aforesaid Power of Attorney by death or otherwise, or notice of any facts indicating the same.

That I hereby represent that the said Principal is now alive; has not, at any time, revoked or repudiated the said Power of Attorney; and the said Power of Attorney is still in full force and effect.

That I make this affidavit for the purpose of inducing (name) to accept delivery of the above-described instrument, as executed by me in my capacity of attorney-in-fact of the said Principal, with the full knowledge that the said (name), in accepting the execution and delivery of the aforesaid instrument and in paying a good and valuable consideration therefor, will rely upon this affidavit.

Sworn to before me on (day, month, year)

Bibliography

Berg, Adriane G. *50 Keys to Avoiding Probate and Reducing Estate Taxes.* Hauppauge, NY: Barron's Educational Series, 1992.

———. *Gifts of Love, The Complete Parents' and Grandparents' Guide to Investing for Children.* South Orange, NJ: Testamentary Press, 1995. (Audiotape course and workbook; Telephone: 1-800-609-2374 Voice Box 2374.)

———. *Warning: Dying May be Hazardous to Your Wealth.* Franklin Lakes, NJ: Career Press, 1995.

———. *Wealthbuilder: A Monthly Investment Guide.* South Orange, NJ: Bochner Family Ltd. Partnership. (Telephone: 1-800-609-2374 Voice Box 2374.)

———, and Arthur Berg Bochner. *The Totally Awesome Business Book for Kids.* New York: Newmarket Press, 1995.

———, and Arthur Berg Bochner. *The Totally Awesome Money Book for Kids and Their Parents.* New York: Newmarket Press, 1993, 1995.

Blum, Laurie. *Free Money for College.* New York: Facts on File, 1993.

Breitbard, Stanley H., and Donna Sammons Carpenter. *The Price Waterhouse Book of Personal Financial Planning.* New York: Henry Holt and Company, 1988.

Cassidy, David J., and Michael J. Alves. *The Scholarship Book.* Englewood Cliffs, NJ: Prentice-Hall, 1990.

Chany, Kalman A., with Geoff Martz. *Student Access Guide to Paying for College.* New York: Random House, 1995.

Foster, Henry, and Doris Freed. *Law and the Family.* New York: Lawyers Cooperative Publishing Company, 1966, Section 29:26, p. 542.

Gordon, Harley, with Jane Daniel. *How to Protect Your Life Savings.* Boston: Financial Planning Institute, 1990.

Griffeth, Bill. *10 Steps to Financial Prosperity.* Chicago, IL: Probus Publishing Company, 1994.

McKee, Cynthia Ruiz, and Phillip C. McKee, Jr. *Cash for College.* New York: Hearst Books, 1993.

Personal and Estate Planning for the Elderly. American Bar Association, 1989.

Sheen, Brian J. *Nest Egg Investing.* New York: G. P. Putnam's Sons, 1987.

Thau, Annette. *The Bond Book.* Chicago: Probus Publishing Company, 1992.

Index

A

abuse, child, 126, 135
accumulation provisions, 45
actual transfer, 20–21
ademption, 129
adoption, 135
    inheritance and, 124, 126
advancements, 16–17
adverse parties, 62
aggressive growth stock funds,
    91
Alabama, 105, 149
alimony, 156. *See also* support
    trusts, 157–59
American Association of
    Community and Junior
    Colleges, 77
American Legion, 82
annuities, 20
Association of Independent
    Colleges and Universities,
    77

B

baccalaureate bonds, 103
Bankers Trust, 53
banks, as trustees, 53–57
Bateman, Maureen, 53
Bochner, Arthur Ross Berg,
    10
Bond Book, The (Thau), 100*n*
bonds:
    baccalaureate, 103
    callable, 102
    corporate, 95, 102
    funds, 92
    inheritance of, 131
    municipal, 92, 95, 102
    savings, 24, 103–4
    treasury, 102
    zero-coupon, 90, 95,
        100–103
Bureau of Public Debt, 104
*Business Week's Guide to
    Mutual Funds,* 92

C

California, 15
callable bonds, 102
Canada, 138
capital gains taxes, 11
  overview of, 18–20
  stepped-up basis and, 18–20
  trusts and, 39, 42
  zero-coupon bonds and,
    101
certificates of deposit (CDs),
  104
  in UGMAs and UTMAs,
    31
Chany, Kalman A., 85–87
charitable contributions, 159
charitable trusts, 112–13
child abuse, 126, 135
child custody, 135–37,
    146–47, 151
child's (2503c) trusts, 58–66
  example of, 164–69
  gift tax exclusion with, 59
  grantor rules for, 61–65
  money borrowed from, 63
  strategy roundups for,
    65–66
child support. *See* support
Cohen, Sally, x–xi
college costs, x, 3–4, 60, 61,
    74–87
  calculation of, 76–79

Chany on, 85–87
direct gifts for, 14
divorce and, 61, 153–54
finance strategies for, 81–85
investments for, 94–98,
    99–107
planning for, 79–85
prepaid programs for,
    105–6
worth of, 74–76
College Sure, 90, 95, 104–5
Colorado, 15
common funds, 54
Connecticut, 126
corporate bonds, 95, 102
creditors:
  FLPs and, 68, 69
  joint accounts and, 25
Crummey provisions, 42–43,
    46–47, 69
custodial accounts. *See*
    Uniform Gifts to Minors
    Accounts; Uniform
    Transfers to Minors
    Accounts
custodians, of bequests, 132
custody, child, 135–37,
    146–47, 151

D

deathbed gifts, 141–42
deductions, tax, 158–59

Delaware, 15
demonstrative bequests, 131
disinheritance, 133
dividend reinvestment
    programs (DRIPs),
    117–19
divorce, 126, 135, 146–60
    college costs and, 61,
        153–54
    court decisions on, 147–50
    decisions on child support
        in, 150–55
    separation agreements and,
        150, 157
    tax consequences of, 155–57
    voluntary payment clauses
        and, 160
dollar-cost averaging, 120
DRIPs (dividend reinvestment
    programs), 117–19

E

Economic Recovery Tax Act
    (ERTA) (1981), 142
education. See college costs
Employee Retirement Income
    Security Act (ERISA),
    50, 51n
equity income funds, 92
ERISA (Employee Retirement
    Income Security Act),
    50, 51n

ERTA (Economic Recovery
    Tax Act) (1981), 142
estate taxes, 4, 11, 13, 19, 20,
    21, 138, 139, 142, 143
    child's trusts and, 59, 60, 61,
        65
    FLPs and, 68, 69
    gift taxes vs., 18
    joint accounts and, 23
    life insurance and, 113, 114
    overview of, 17–18
    trusts and, 36, 40, 42
exemptions, tax, 157

F

failed bequests, 129
family limited partnerships
    (FLPs), 67–69
    college aid and, 86
    example of, 170–71
financial aid, 85–87, 96
financial-aid forms, 153–54
fixed income funds, 92
flexible variable life insurance,
    109–10
FLPs. See family limited
    partnerships
Form 8615, 162
Form 8814, 162, 163
Foster, Henry, 137
foster care, 135
401(k) plans, 84–85

Friedland Fishbein Laifer & Robbins, 69

G

general durable powers of attorney, 71–72
generation-skipping tax, 143, 145
generation-skipping trusts, 143–45
gifting. *See also specific topics*
  actual transfer in, 20–21
  establishing goals in, 1–9
  out-of-date notions about, 141–43
  outright, 8–9
  profile of, 5
  style of, 6–8
gift splitting, 14
gift taxes, 11, 141, 142
  child's trusts and, 59, 65
  estate taxes vs., 18
  filing of, 15
  gift splitting and, 14
  overview of, 13–17
  state, 15
  trusts and, 40, 43, 47
grandparents:
  and gifting to grandchildren, 139–45
  responsibilities of, 138
  rights of, 134–37

grantor trusts, 61–65
"gross-up" provisions, 142
growth and income funds, 92
guardians, 133

H

Harvard University, 75
Howell, Martha, ix–x
Howell, Richard, ix–x

I

Ibbotson, 90, 109
illegitimate children, 126
income taxes, 4, 11, 20, 21
  See also capital gains taxes; kiddie tax
  child's trusts and, 61, 62
  and gifting to grandchildren, 139
  on minors, 11–13
  trusts and, 36–37, 42
index funds, 91
Individual Retirement Accounts (IRAs), 83–84, 87
  for minors, 12
inheritance. *See also* estate taxes
  children's rights and, 123–25
  divorce and, 154–55

parents' rights and, 125–26

per capita vs. per stirpes, 127–28

preparing children for, 122–33

insurance policies. *See also* life insurance

in UGMAs, 30

inter vivos trusts, 37–38, 144

in trust for (ITF) accounts, 25

investment options, 88–98

investment plans, 89–90

IRAs. *See* Individual Retirement Accounts

ITF (in trust for) accounts, 25

J

James, Rosie, 53

joint accounts, 22–27

popular misconceptions about, 23

potential tax problems with, 25–27

types of, 24

K

Keogh accounts, 83–84

kiddie tax, 12

Form 8615 for, 162

trusts and, 60

on UGMAs and UTMAs, 30

L

large cap stock funds, 92

letters precatory, 129–30

life insurance, 107, 108–16

charitable trusts with, 112–13

choosing among, 115–16

flexible variable, 109–10

paid-up, 116

paying premiums of, with cash policy value, 116

renewable term, 113–14

straight (whole), 114–15

survivorship whole, 110–12

universal, 108–9

limited powers of attorney, 72

loans, ix–x

student, 83

Louisiana, 15

lump-sum planning, 99–107

M

McPherson, M. Peter, 76

Making the Most of Your Money (Quinn), 108

Making Up for Lost Time (Berg), 108

medical costs, 60

direct gifts for, 14

divorce and, 159

medical school, ix–x

Michigan State University,
75–76
military, college costs and,
81–82
Minnesota, 15
minor's trusts. *See* child's
trusts
Money, 74
money market accounts, 92,
120
Money Show, The, ix
municipal bonds, 92, 95, 102
funds of, 92
mutual funds, 91–93
dollar-cost averaging with,
120
in UGMAs, 30

N

National Association of State
Universities and Land
Grant Colleges, 77
National Insurance
Consumers Organization
(NICO), 114
New Mexico, 105
New School for Social
Research, 122
New York State, 15, 17, 126
NICO (National Insurance
Consumers
Organization), 114

nondurable powers of
attorney, 72
North Carolina, 15

O

Ohio, 105
Oklahoma, 15
Omnibus Budget
Reconciliation Act (1993),
35, 58
Oregon, 15

P

parental rights, 125–26
payable on death (POD)
accounts, 25
per capita inheritance, 127
per stirpes inheritance, 127–28
POD (payable on death)
accounts, 25
"pot" trusts, 133
powers of attorney, 70–73
examples of, 172–77
types of, 71–73
*Princeton Review Student
Access Guide to Paying for
College, The* (Chany), 86
probate, joint accounts and,
22, 23, 25, 27
property transfers, in divorce,
157

prudent person rule, 97–98
Puerto Rico, 15

Q

Quinn, Jane Bryant, 108

R

real estate, 24
    college costs paid with,
        106–7
renewable term life insurance,
    113–14
Reserve Officers' Training
    Corps (ROTC), 81–82
residency, colleges and, 81
retirement accounts, 83–85.
    See also Individual
    Retirement Accounts
Rhode Island, 15
ROTC (Reserve Officers'
    Training Corps), 81–82
Rudenstine, Neil, 75

S

S&P 500 index funds, 91
savings bonds, U.S., 24,
    103–4
Scudder, 77, 119
securities. *See also* bonds;
    stocks

in UGMAs and UTMAs, 30,
    31
separation agreements, 150,
    157
single trusts, 133
small cap stock funds, 91, 92
South Carolina, 15
spendthrift provisions, 44–45
springing powers of attorney,
    73
state laws:
    on inheritance, 123–24,
        154
    on support, 149, 152
    on trusts, 34, 41
    on UGMAs and UTMAs,
        28, 30
    on visitation, 136
stepped-up basis, 18–20, 39
stocks, 90–94
    DRIPs with, 117–19
    inheritance of, 131–32
    joint purchase of, 24
straight life insurance, 114–15
student loans, 83
support, 146–60
    budgets in determination
        of, 151–53
    court decisions on, 147–50
    decision-making about,
        150–55
    tax consequences of, 155–57
    unallocated, 156–57

support *(continued)*
  voluntary payment clauses
    and, 160
survivorship whole life
  insurance, 110–12

T

taxes. *See also* capital gains
  taxes; estate taxes; gift
  taxes; income taxes;
  kiddie tax; *specific topics*
  on children's assets, 10–21
  congressional plans for, 16
  deductions on, 158–59
  exemptions on, 157
  flow charts for, 162–63
Tax Reform Act (1986), 12
Tennessee, 15
testamentary trusts, 37, 38,
  49, 51, 132–33, 144
Thau, Annette, 100*n*
throwbacks, 45
*Totally Awesome Money
  Book for Kids and Their
  Parents, The* (Berg),
  118–19
Totten trusts, 25
treasury bills, 95
treasury bonds, 102
trustees, 48–57
  costs of, 56
  criteria for, 53

institutions vs. individuals
  as, 49–57
trusts, 33–43. *See also* child's
  trusts
  accumulation provisions
    in, 45
  alimony, 157–59
  capital gains tax savings
    from, 39, 42
  charitable, 112–13
  college aid and, 86
  continuity in crisis from, 39
  Crummey provisions in,
    42–43, 46–47, 69
  definition of, 34
  establishment of, 40–43
  estate tax savings from, 36,
    40, 42
  generation-skipping,
    143–45
  gifting to, 15–16
  gift tax and, 40, 43, 47
  grantor, 61–65
  inter vivos, 37–38, 144
  irrevocable vs. revocable, 35
  prioritizing goals of, 41–43
  professional management
    of, 38–39, 42
  selecting trustees for, 48–57
  single ("pot"), 133
  spendthrift provisions in,
    44–45
  types of, 37–38

2503c trusts. *See* child's trusts
two-year colleges, 81

U

unified gift and estate tax
    credit, 15
Uniform Gifts to Minors
    Accounts (UGMAs),
    28–32, 58, 59, 65
  college aid and, 86
  pros and cons of, 31–32
Uniform Transfers to Minors
    Accounts (UTMAs),
    29–32, 58, 59, 65
  college aid and, 86
  pros and cons of, 31–32
universal life insurance, 108–9
U.S. News & World Report, 75

V

Vermont, 15
Veterans Administration, 82
Virginia, 15

visitation rights, 136–37
voluntary payment clauses,
    160

W

WABC, ix
Washington State, 15
"Wealthbuilder," 161
whole life insurance, 114–15
wills, 16–17, 123, 124
  divorce and, 154–55
  minor children in, 132–33
  preparation of, 126–28
  provisions of, 128–33
  testamentary trusts and, 37,
    38, 49, 51, 132–33, 144
Wisconsin, 15
Wyoming, 105

Z

zero-coupon bonds, 90, 95,
    100–103

An Open Invitation

For many parents and grandparents, a family limited partnership or one of the many types of trusts described in this book will be in order. For others, tax reduction, will-writing, asset protection, estate planning, and probate avoidance will be a priority. You are invited to write to the law firm for which I act as counsel. They will send you, without charge, additional materials on asset protection that you may use with your attorneys: Friedland Fishbein Laifer & Robbins, 233 Broadway, New York, NY 10279.

As readers of this book, no matter where you live, you may also take advantage of a special invitation to work with them through the same streamlined, economical program that I offer to my radio listeners in New York, New Jersey, and Connecticut. Call (212) 962-4888, or write *Wealthbuilder*, 71 Valley Street, Suite 300, South Orange, NJ 07079.

Sincerely,
Adriane G. Berg

P.S. Everyone who writes or calls will also receive three full months of my asset protection and investment newsletter *Wealthbuilder*. It will keep you up to date on late-breaking news in law, investing, and financial planning.

About the Author

Adriane G. Berg, an attorney and editor of *Wealthbuilder,* a monthly financial guide, hosts *The Money Show* weekly for WABC radio. She is also the author of numerous articles and nineteen books including her best-selling *Financial Planning for Couples: How to Work Together to Build Security and Success, Your Wealth-Building Years: Financial Planning for 18- to 38-Year-Olds* and, with her son, Arthur Bochner, *The Totally Awesome Money Book for Kids* and *The Totally Awesome Business Book for Kids.* An expert in taxation, estate planning, asset protection, and global business development, Berg has appeared on *The Oprah Winfrey Show, Good Morning America, The Maury Povich Show, Sally Jessy Raphaël,* and other shows to discuss money matters. A much sought-after speaker, she has conducted and designed seminars for IDS Financial Services, Prudential Securities, Kirlin Securities, and Interstate Financial Group, among many others. Currently of counsel to the law firm of Friedland Fishbein Laifer & Robbins, Adriane G. Berg lives in New Jersey with her family.